Memory Power

MEMORY POWER

Ursula Markham

VERMILION
London

To Philip and David
With all my love

Published in 1993 by Vermilion
an imprint of The Random House Group
Random House
20 Vauxhall Bridge Road
London SW1V 2SA

Second impression 1993

Catalogue record for this book is available
from the British Library.

ISBN 0 091775787

Typeset in Baskerville by Hope Services (Abingdon) Ltd.
Printed and bound in Great Britain by
Mackays of Chatham PLC, Chatham, Kent

Contents

No man can reveal to you aught but that which already lies half asleep in the dawning of your knowledge.

The Prophet, Kahlil Gibran

Introduction

Are you a student at college or university? A businessman or – woman who realises the value in money terms of being able to remember information accurately at will? Are you returning to work after a long absence, or do you become embarrassed when you have problems matching names to faces? Perhaps you would like to study a new subject simply for the pleasure of it but are deterred by the thought that you might have difficulty in absorbing the knowledge to begin with, and in recalling it later?

If you can answer yes to any of these questions – or if you simply want to know how to increase your learning ability and improve your memory – this book is for you.

It does not set out to confound you with science or to list all the wonderful discoveries made about the human brain during the last few decades. You will be shown practical and effective ways of boosting your learning power and applying it to real life. You will find, throughout, simple exercises you can practise so that, before you have even finished reading the book, you will have been able to prove to yourself that these methods work.

You're entering a fascinating and limitless world – enjoy it.

1
Brain Power

You may have heard it said that we only use about 8 per cent of the brain's potential. In fact some psychologists would now claim that we use no more than 4 per cent; but even if we take the former figure, that means that 92 per cent of the brain's capacity is lying unused. When you think of all the knowledge and information you have acquired over the years, just imagine how much more you would know if you could manage to harness even half of that unused portion.

Why is it that so little of the brain's potential is used? The simple answer is that, until recently, no one has really known much about how it functions. As this knowledge increases we become more able to develop our own brain power.

You may be thinking that you had lessons in a wide variety of different academic subjects when you were at school and you did very well, thank you. But how much of what you were taught can you remember now? Be honest. Unless you have maintained a particular interest in a subject, you are likely to have forgotten more than you remember. And yet there are many things which you were never formally taught which you are able to recall with no difficulty whatsoever. You have not forgotten the date of your birthday or how to tell the time. I am sure you know your own address and the names of your children. Why is this? Because these facts have been learned *creatively*; that is, not by constantly repeating words parrot-fashion but by absorbing them naturally and relating them to real life and what is important to you without consciously making the effort to do so.

What is learning?

True learning has nothing at all to do with the automatic repetition of facts – even though this is how most of us were taught at school. Learning consists of three things:

1. The absorption of new ideas (which naturally involves being able to understand them)
2. Blending these new ideas with those you already have in order to enhance and extend your field of knowledge
3. Being sufficiently comfortable with those ideas to be able to explain them to other people should the occasion arise

The two halves of the brain

Your brain is divided into two halves, left and right. It has been known for some time that the left side of the brain governs the right side of the body, and that the right side of the brain governs the left side of the body. This means that damage to the left side of the brain can cause paralysis to the right half of the body, and vice versa.

In the last quarter-century, however, researchers have also been able to show that each side of the brain deals with separate and different mental functions. Two of the best known of these researchers are Dr Robert Ornstein and Dr Roger Sperry of the University of California, whose work in this field won them a Nobel prize. Before we go on to look at which half of the brain governs which mental activities, take a moment to answer 'yes' or 'no' to the following questions:

1. I have an artistic nature
2. I have always been a daydreamer
3. I love listening to/playing music
4. I have a vivid imagination
5. I dream in pictures
6. I have a good sense of rhythm

7. I like to know the reason for everything
8. I have always had an aptitude for figures
9. I am a logical thinker
10. I like to use the right word in the right place
11. Scientific subjects fascinate me
12. I like to deal with one thing at a time

If you answered mostly 'yes' to questions 1–6 and 'no' to 7–12, you are predominantly right-brained. If the reverse is true, you are predominantly left-brained. Because of the way in which formal education is usually conducted, I would expect most readers to be left-brained. The ideal, however, is to achieve a perfect balance between the two.

The diagram below illustrates the functions of the two halves of the brain:

Left brain	*Right brain*
reasoning	intuition
logic	artistic ability
analysis	music/rhythm
one thing at a time	imagination
use of language	dreams/daydreams
mathematics	visual recognition
calculation	facial expression
memory of words and numbers	tone of voice/body language
	dealing with several things at once

Looking at this diagram, it does not take long to see that most of us were brought up to be left-brained. Indeed, for many people right-brain activity was actually quashed when they were told: 'Concentrate' or 'Don't daydream'. Of course we all need left-brain capabilities – it is necessary to be able to reason and to understand figures – but it is important that the right brain should be allowed to develop too or we will soon forget how to use it. The good news is that such a state of affairs is not final; we can learn to reactivate the right brain. Even better news is that, in the course of their research, Ornstein and Sperry found that when we use the two halves of our brain we are not just doubling our mental ability but increasing it up to ten times.

You already use your right brain more than you may realise. It is the right brain which helps you to take in the whole picture when you are introduced to somebody new. The left brain would simply register the hairstyle, the colour of the eyes, the shape of the chin and so on.

Modern society has come to place a greater emphasis and more value on left-brain functioning. The scientist is thought to be cleverer and more 'valuable' than the artist; the doctor than the musician. However, the development of either side of the brain can improve the functioning of the other. It certainly is not true that to excel in one automatically means that one is weak in the other. Think of Leonardo da Vinci; think of Einstein.

One of the aims of this book is to encourage you to think creatively (that is, in a right-brained way), thereby improving your ability to acquire knowledge of what you may hitherto have considered to be left-brain subjects.

Brain function and age

It used to be thought that mental ability automatically decreased as we grew older. It was believed that the brain reached its peak when we were between eighteen and twenty-five years old and thereafter deteriorated so that we became less able to learn or remember. This is just not true.

Professor Mark Rosenweig of the University of California proved that (provided it was not damaged by accident or injury) the brain can continue to develop at any age provided sufficient stimulation is given. To emphasise the fact that the brain can still function efficiently and well even among octogenarians we only have to think of such people as Michelangelo, Goethe, Picasso, Bertrand Russell, Einstein and George Bernard Shaw.

It is true that a certain number of our brain cells are destroyed as we grow older. But research has indicated that we have so many to start with that, even if we were to lose 10,000 every single day, we would lose less than 5 per cent of those cells by the end of our lives.

While mental ability does not necessarily decrease with age, it *is* a fact that the body itself deteriorates. If arteries become clogged, then less oxygen is able to reach the brain. It has been shown that, when their arteries have been medically cleared, not only do patients become less stressed and agitated but their IQ actually increases. In addition, although it is accepted that high blood pressure often accompanies loss of mental agility, it is now also known that improved mental functioning returns when the blood pressure decreases.

For these reasons, exercise and nutrition are important, as is the taking of regular breaks when you are engaged in concentrated mental work. Later in this book you will be shown some breathing and relaxation exercises designed to increase the flow of oxygen to the brain and thus help you to improve your memory and mental functioning.

External influences on the brain

Nutrition

You may have read some of the recent reports stating that children whose diet consisted largely of junk food did not do as well in intelligence tests as children whose diet was healthier. Those same reports claimed that, when the first group of children were given supplements in the form of extra vitamins and minerals, their performance improved considerably.

The children in the first group were not, then, necessarily less intelligent than those in the second group. They were, however, not able to function to the best of their individual ability.

The same is true of all of us throughout our lives. If you want to improve your own learning power, don't you owe it to yourself to see that you start with the greatest possible advantage? I am not suggesting that you become fanatical about this; provided your diet is basically healthy (and that you do not suffer from any particular medical condition or allergy), the occasional lapse into self-indulgence will do you no harm at all.

There is more to it than ensuring you have all the correct vitamins and minerals. Practitioners of Ayurvedic medicine (the traditional form of Indian medicine) believe that:

1. a high intake of high-fat foods induces depression and lethargy
2. an excess of meat or highly spiced food can cause aggressive tendencies
3. a diet which is high in pulses, fresh vegetables and rice leads to the clearest mental state

Ayurvedic medicine is centuries old but is increasingly practised in the Western world today. And many modern nutritionists have also come to accept the effect of the food we eat on our mental faculties.

While it is naturally beneficial, for many different reasons, to reduce one's weight to a reasonable level, care should be taken that the weight-loss regime is not too drastic, especially when following a course of study at the same time. As anyone who has followed a stringent diet will be aware, irritation, headaches and lack of concentration are often the result.

Stimulants

You might imagine that the caffeine contained in both tea and coffee could give you that extra boost to help you remain alert when studying. However, this is only true in the very short term. Before long, the caffeine will produce symptoms of stress which will in fact be counter-productive. Remember how difficult it is to think clearly when under stress, and you will realise the effect that an excess of caffeine will have upon your ability to absorb and recall information. The occasional cup of either beverage is unlikely to do any great harm; the problems arise when you feel unable to study at all without a strong cup of coffee at your elbow.

Alcohol

While I am not advocating strict abstention, it must be remembered that alcohol and alertness simply do not mix. In the short term, alcohol is likely to make you lethargic and less able to concentrate. Long-term problems are more serious: over-indulgence can cause permanent loss of memory function. This becomes more serious as we grow older, and it has been shown that excessive alcohol does in fact lead to premature aging of the brain.

Tobacco

We have all read and heard a great deal about the harmful effects of tobacco, but what people often do not realise is that smoking actually reduces the amount of oxygen being carried to the brain at any given moment. This results in the smoker being less able to think clearly. In addition, repeated tests carried out in both the United States and Britain have indicated that non-smokers have demonstrably better powers of recall than those who smoke.

Drugs

Both prescribed and non-prescription drugs may mar mental ability. If you are a hay-fever sufferer, you will already know that the antihistamines you take to relieve the symptoms often cause you to feel drowsy and to lose concentration – and in fact usually carry a warning not to operate potentially dangerous machinery immediately after taking them. Other medication may well cause your reactions to become slower or may induce feelings of despondency. If your medication is prescribed and therefore necessary, there is not a great deal you can do about it, apart from being aware that your mind may not be as clear, or your reflexes as sharp, while you are taking it.

Non-prescribed substances bring their own problems – forgetting for the moment the harmful effects on your general health and concentrating only on the damage they may do to your powers of learning. Not only is actual mental ability measurably reduced but judgment is usually impaired at the same time, leading the individual to *believe* that he or she is functioning better than usual when the reverse is, in fact, the case.

Exercise

Among its other benefits, regular physical exercise improves the circulation and this in turn results in oxygen being carried quickly and more easily to the brain. (This is the reason for the sense of elation often experienced immediately after a period of fairly strenuous exercise.) The brain is therefore able to function more effectively and, even though your arms and legs may ache, your ability to learn is likely to be enhanced.

Conditioning

Each of us is a product of conditioning which began at the moment we entered this world. A series of people and circumstances have influenced us and the way we feel about ourselves – whether that feeling is positive or negative. Such conditioning is often not deliberately inflicted, but the effects are real and long-lasting none the less.

Once this conditioning is in place, we are often our own worst enemies when it comes to continuing the process. Each of us erects our own barriers in life – often without realising we are doing it. Take, for example, the adult who claims: 'I can't speak French. I was never any good at learning foreign languages.' Had that person been born in

France, the offspring of French parents, they would have been chattering away in that language by the age of three! Same person – same brain. So it cannot be that he or she is not capable of speaking French – only that they *believe* this to be the case. They have erected their own barrier and they alone can tear it down.

If learning a language is one of the problems you face – and it applies to so many people at the present time – think of just how a child begins to speak. Not for him the conjugation of dozens of irregular verbs or the study of adverbial clauses. The child will begin by pointing at things and uttering a single noun. 'Book,' he will say or, when a little more advanced, 'Want book.' Now I am not suggesting that the businessman about to embark on trade with the European market will wish to be quite so crude in his application of the new language, but it certainly makes more sense for him to concentrate initially on those words and phrases which are likely to prove most useful. Once he has mastered those and has become confident in their use, there is ample time to progress to a deeper study of the construction of the language.

Take time to look at yourself, your past, and the good and bad influences on your life. Try to understand the person you have become and how you think about your brain power. Look at your positive and negative aspects and see if you can discover why they exist. Don't spend time regretting the past or being bitter – it's such a waste of energy which could be far more profitably employed. Just make sure that your past conditioning does not exert too strong an influence on your future. You have the right to begin to take charge of your own life.

Stress

Have you ever had your mind 'go blank' just as you were about to speak? Has there been an occasion when you have been unable to call to mind a name or fact which you know quite well? If you can answer 'yes' to either of these questions, it is quite likely that the lapse occurred at the worst possible time – just when you wanted to make a point or when everyone was looking at you and waiting to hear what you were about to say.

Such temporary lapses of memory are often caused by stress or nervous tension. And you would have to be Superman (or -woman) not to feel a certain element of nervousness just before making a presentation or sitting an exam. It has nothing to do with how well you know your subject. It is just that this natural nervousness creates stress and this in turn creates anxiety. And there you are, trapped in a vicious circle from which there seems no escape – indeed, the harder you try to think clearly at such times, the more difficult it may be to achieve.

If you find yourself in this position, there is much to be said for a few moments of deep breathing to relieve the pressure and reduce the panic. However, the best way of counteracting such stress is to take preventative measures. Let us suppose, for example, that you have been asked to give a talk to a local organisation. Here is a simple routine you might like to follow:

1. You need to begin some time in advance of the actual event – two or three weeks beforehand is the ideal starting time. This is when you should start to practise a relaxation technique. You might decide to use one of the many audio cassettes on the market (for details of these, see the information section on p. 158); you might attend a yoga class; or you might simply try the relaxation exercise described on p. 68. Not only will you find this exercise a pleasant way of passing ten minutes each day, but you will actually be lowering your blood pressure and releasing much of the tension from your muscles at the same time.

2. Continue to practise your chosen relaxation technique daily until the day of the talk.

3. Practise it again on the morning of the talk itself and then, just before you are due to begin, simply take a few deep breaths and picture your perfect place in your mind. You don't need to close your eyes, and no one will realise what you are doing, but your subconscious will automatically make the link between the familiar

image and the feeling of relaxation and much of the tension will leave you. This in turn will prevent you from experiencing those temporary but embarrassing lapses in memory once you begin.

Setting the scene

So you have decided that you want to learn something – or perhaps it is necessary for you to do so. It seems only sensible to make things as easy as possible for yourself by making your surroundings as suitable and comfortable as you can and by going about the whole process in the way most likely to create success.

Where you learn

If you are spending a great deal of time studying, then ideally you should try to have a space reserved just for that purpose, such as a desk or table which is not going to be used for other things. But this is not an ideal world and it may be that the only place you can find is the kitchen or dining-room table. But you can make sure that you have a chair which is firm but comfortable – and which is the right height for you. Nothing is going to put you off studying more than a seat which makes your legs or your back ache. There are some people who like to study while sitting on the floor or in an armchair. But, if you are attempting any serious form of learning, sitting at a desk or table is usually better than curling up in the corner of the sofa. Not only does it give you space should you need to spread out books and papers, but it shows that you mean business, helps to put you in the appropriate frame of mind – and makes it less likely that you'll fall asleep! In addition, even though you may find the discipline unnatural in the beginning, your subconscious mind will soon get used to the idea that this is the place for study.

Try and keep your desk or table as uncluttered as possible. Obviously you will need certain books, paper, pens and so on, but if the whole surface is covered with books, scraps of paper and old coffee mugs you will find it far more difficult to concentrate. And the presence of all that clutter is likely to create a feeling of stress within you – which is just what we are trying to avoid.

Comfort

The more comfortable you are, the less you will have to distract you. The temperature of the room should be warm enough for comfort but not so warm that you soon begin to feel sleepy. Make sure there is sufficient fresh air, too; if it is the middle of winter and too cold to open a window, perhaps you could try using a fan – or even getting up every now and then and stepping outside for a few deep breaths. Stale, stuffy air is likely to make you feel drowsy.

Your clothes should be comfortable, too. If your belt is too tight or your shoes pinch, take them off. Clothing which is light and warm and fairly loose-fitting is best.

Know yourself

Are you a lark or an owl? Do you find it easier to think clearly first thing in the morning or very late at night? Where feasible, try and arrange your study time to suit your personality. There is no point in making things as difficult as possible for yourself, so it is worth making a few changes in your daily routine in order to fit your 'learning time' into your most alert time of day.

You may be one of those people who can only study in complete silence, or you may like a background of music. Neither of these is right or wrong; it is simply a case of thinking about yourself and how you prefer to function. If you do decide to use music, however, it is best to choose something which does not have words as these will intrude upon your consciousness and may impede your progress. It can be helpful to use the same piece of music as your background each time you study, as this is another way of putting your subconscious in the right frame of mind.

Plan your time

Nothing is easier than postponing your study periods – particularly if hard work is involved or you think you are going to find it difficult. So plan your learning time – but do be realistic about it. It is far better to promise yourself that you will devote one hour a day to your studies, and then keep that promise, than it is to start off in true January 1st style by vowing to study for four hours a day, only to let yourself down by day three (or even sooner).

Take breaks

It might sound oh-so-virtuous to claim that you worked for eight hours without a break but, even if it were true, you would not be doing yourself any favours. For one thing, you will never keep it up, and for another, you will soon be so exhausted that nothing you read will really sink in. Indeed, the eminent French expert Henri Pieron found that we are more likely to be able to recall what we have learned if we take a break every thirty minutes or so.

And a break has to be a *real* break. Don't just sit at your desk doing nothing. Get up and walk about. Have a drink, play with the cat or water the plants. Whatever you do need only take about five minutes or so, but the benefits will be quite noticeable. You will return to your desk refreshed and more able to assimilate further knowledge.

It has also been recognised that we remember best those facts we learn at the start and finish of each session. Look at the diagrams below, and you will see that the 'paragon' who studies for three hours without a break only has two areas of peak recall.

Now suppose our virtuous student had broken the periods of study into half-hour sessions.

There would now be twelve periods of peak recall ability – at the beginning and end of each session.

None of the suggestions given above is going to take the place of real effort on your part but, by putting them into practice, you will be making things as easy and comfortable for yourself as possible. In Chapter 2 we will go on to look

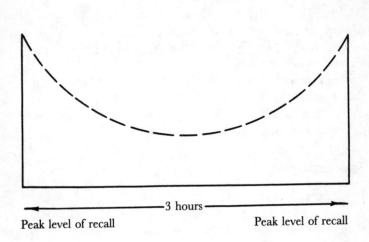

─────3 hours─────

Peak level of recall　　　　　　　Peak level of recall

at ways of thinking more creatively and therefore acquiring knowledge with less effort than you may previously have thought necessary.

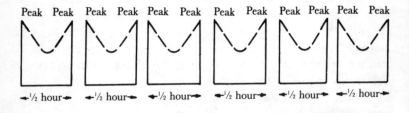

2
Creative Thinking

In Chapter 1 you answered a list of twelve questions designed to give you some indication of whether you are predominantly left- or right-brained. To discover a little more about yourself and about the way you think, see what you make of this:

$$1 + 1 =$$

The most obvious solution to this is the one which probably sprang first to mind, i.e. $1 + 1 = 2$. And that answer is, of course, correct. That is to say it is *one* of the possible correct answers. There are several others, including:

$$1 + 1 = 11$$
$$1 + 1 = T$$
$$1 + 1 = X$$
$$1 + 1 = L$$
$$1 + 1 = V$$

and so on. . . .

The obvious answer is reached by an analytical or non-creative thought process. The others are the result of creative or imaginative thinking. The creative thinker uses his or her imagination to look at the question from all angles and to come up with as many solutions as possible. The non-creative (left-brained) thinker, however, only has one relatively narrow viewpoint.

Creative thinking is something you can develop in yourself – although it will take practice, as our Western upbringing does not encourage us to use our minds in this way. And the way in which you think can affect any aspect of your life, whether you are a student or have a business to run and decisions to make.

Here is another test for you to try. Give yourself two minutes to write down all the uses you can think of for a metal knitting needle. Do it now before reading any further.

Well, how did you do? Most people when faced with this particular test are able to list anything from two to twenty uses, with the majority averaging about eight. Using creative thinking, you should be able to list as many as you are physically capable of writing down within the given time. A student in one of my seminars actually managed to give 113 answers – although his handwriting was somewhat difficult to decipher! These answers included the obvious, such as knitting; the fairly sensible, supporting the stem of a pot plant; and the downright ridiculous. But then, no one ever said they had to be sensible applications for the knitting needle, simply possible ones.

Here are just a few of the answers he gave. Perhaps they will lead you to think of some more of your own:

- extracting juice from a lemon by piercing the skin of the fruit with the point of the needle
- applying a tourniquet
- holding up hair which has been twisted into a bun or knot
- as a pole for a paper flag
- as a splint for a dog's leg
- repairing broken knicker elastic
- clearing drains
- picking up litter
- dipping in ink to use as a makeshift pen

You will see from the sample list given above that creative thought involves stretching the mind and the imagination as far as possible. By doing this in relatively light-hearted exercises you will be helping your mind to become accustomed to doing more than follow the rigid thought patterns so familiar to most of us. This, in turn, will prove helpful to you when you engage in the learning process.

Brainstorming

One particularly effective use of creative thinking is brainstorming. This is not a new concept, having been devised in the United States in the 1930s by Alex Osborn. Over the years, however, the true meaning of the word has become clouded and it is generally thought to mean nothing more than a group of people sitting around and coming up with ideas. But this is only a small part of the actual process; there are certain essential points to bear in mind during a brainstorming session:

1. At least eight to ten people should be involved in a session if it is to work effectively − although there can be as many as twenty provided the session leader is able to control proceedings.

2. A session leader is chosen whose job is to state the problem initially and then to restate it at regular intervals. He should also ensure that someone writes down all the ideas as they arise. As you will see, some of these ideas will be so novel (or so outrageous) that, if no one writes them down, they are likely to be lost for ever. The leader must also see that each member of the group receives an equal opportunity to state ideas, or all the running will be made by the more openly extrovert.

3. The problem is written down and placed where it is in full view for the whole session.

4. The session leader turns the problem into a question (usually beginning 'How can we . . . ?') For example, he might tell the group that the company's profits have fallen during the past year and ask, 'How can we increase profits in the next six months?'

5. The session is thrown open to the whole group and everyone is encouraged to put forward as many ideas as possible within a designated time. The important point to remember − and this is where creative thinking comes in − is that *all* ideas are welcome, whether they are sensible, unusual or even ridiculous. No one is allowed to turn on the proposer of a solution and tell them that

their idea is stupid or unworkable; sensible evaluation comes later.

6. At the end of the allotted time, the leader draws the session to a close, and consideration of *every* suggestion noted begins.

You will appreciate, after reading the description above, that a brainstorming session is not the quiet and solemn affair of which business meetings are normally made. There is usually a fair amount of laughter and noise as suggestions are called out from one and all. But this is a good thing as it is this uninhibited atmosphere which encourages spontaneous and creative thought.

7. Now it is time for the leader to introduce a little more seriousness to the session, as evaluation of the ideas begins. (It might be necessary to have a five-minute break between the first and second halves of the session in order to get participants into a less hilarious frame of mind.) The group then considers each suggestion in turn, no matter how unworkable or inappropriate it may appear. It is surprising how often a seemingly ridiculous thought, with a little sensible adaptation, can become a feasible proposition. After all, if your dog had a broken leg and the only thing around was a knitting needle, you would be quite happy to use it as a temporary splint, wouldn't you?

Some years ago one of the major high street building societies held a brainstorming session, during which one of the questions posed was: 'How are we to encourage parents with young children to come and consult our financial advisers?' In addition to the sensible ideas others were put forward, such as 'Put all the children in a giant playpen' and 'Tie the children to the chairs.' It was only a short step from such ideas to the miniature tables and chairs now found in many banks and building societies, some equipped with building bricks and others with toy telephones connected to automatic recordings of children's stories.

Brainstorming can be an effective process, whether we are talking about an organisation faced with a corporate decision or an individual trying to decide upon his or her direction in life. Remember that the idea is to accumulate as many ideas as possible – from the intelligent to the ridiculous – within a given period of time. The more outlandish of them can be discarded later.

Creative thinking often involves the linking together of hitherto unrelated ideas, something which frequently occurs when jokes or amusing anecdotes are told – the different points only come together at the punchline. In addition, creative thinking involves turning preconceptions on their heads. Consider the following tale:

It is seven o'clock in the morning. Breakfast is on the table and the mother goes into her son's bedroom. 'Jimmy, get up! You'll be late for school. Your breakfast is ready.' Jimmy turns over in bed and grunts.

Ten minutes later the mother goes again into her son's room. Now she is angry. 'Get out of bed!' she shouts. 'You're going to be late.'

Jimmy opens his eyes and looks at his mother. 'I don't want to go to school today,' he says. 'There are a thousand pupils at school and I know they all hate me. There are twenty teachers there and they all hate me too. Give me one good reason why I should go.'

'I'll give you two reasons,' replies his mother. 'One, you're forty-five years old, and two, you're the headmaster.'

The only thing which makes the story amusing is the surprise, at the end, that we are dealing with a forty-five-year-old man – and the headmaster at that. Yet nowhere in the story is it said that it concerns a child. Our own preconceptions lead us to that belief. Because we automatically link school with children and because the idea of a mother waking her son makes us think of a schoolboy, we *assume* that this is what we are dealing with. Creative thinking asks you to forget your preconceptions and to avoid making assumptions, and this is precisely what the great thinkers have done throughout the ages. Original thought does not stem from a mind full of bias.

Self-imposed barriers

Because of our upbringing and the fact that we are led to become predominantly left-brained, we have a tendency to put barriers in our own paths when it comes to creative thinking.

1. We assume that there is only one correct answer to any given problem. You have already seen that this is not so. There may turn out to be one answer which is better than the others, but the others do exist.

2. We are afraid of appearing foolish. This is why brain-storming sessions where you are positively encouraged to say the first thing that comes into your head – however ridiculous it may be – are so beneficial. If the opportunity does not arise for you to be part of a brain-storming group, why not spend two minutes each day inventing as many uses as possible for any ordinary household item you care to choose? It would encourage you to think creatively and to forget the whole idea of foolishness.

3. Many people are nervous of doing things in a way which is different from that which they consider 'normal'. Surely this cannot apply to you. You have presumably decided that you wish to extend the boundaries of your thinking in order to learn more easily and improve your memory. If that is not the case, why are you reading this book?

4. Fear of failure. Failing is something we all have to face from time to time, and it can be the most precious of gifts if approached in the right way. There is the world of difference between 'failing' at something and 'being a failure'. The former is part of a learning process, while the latter is a negative attitude of mind. Watch a small child learning how to walk and see how many times he falls down. Does he think to himself: 'I have fallen down. I am a failure. I cannot walk'? No, he picks himself up and tries again, perhaps learning as he does so that it is important to keep his balance. If a tiny child can do it, so can you.

5. Being easily deterred by obstacles. An obstacle can be an insurmountable problem or it can simply cause you to rethink. An airline pilot setting out on a flight from London to Los Angeles will have plotted his route and know precisely where he is heading. But difficulties may arise along the way. A passenger may be taken seriously ill, a fault may develop in the engine of the aircraft, or he may encounter freak weather conditions. So what does he do? He may have to change his route, make an unscheduled landing or delay his journey. But he doesn't just sit in the cabin of his craft on the runway at Heathrow and tell himself that he will never get to Los Angeles. He rethinks his plans, taking the obstacles into account, and makes new decisions accordingly.

Any business executive may spend hours working on a plan designed to increase the company turnover in the coming year, only to find that plan thwarted by matters beyond his control. A supplier may go into liquidation, a strike may occur or any number of other problems may arise. Our executive then has two choices: he (or she) can sit at his desk, head in hands and bemoan his bad luck; or he can use a combination of acquired knowledge and creative thought to find a way round the problems.

6. Automatic rejection of an idea which may appear in any way 'different'. If this applies to you, recognise it as something which results from your earliest programming; recognise also that you have the right to choose for yourself, whether or not you allow it to be part of your way of thinking in the future. Without ideas which are different, how would anything practical ever be invented or any work of art created?

7. A tendency to make snap decisions. Now there are times when an instant decision is essential; if you are standing in the road and you see a huge lorry bearing down upon you, you need to decide pretty quickly what you want to do. And, of course, there are occasions when that first, instinctive reaction is going to be the right one. But that does not mean you should not, in general, take the time to evaluate other ideas: you may well glean something beneficial from them, even if you *do* decide your first idea was best.

8. Taking the easiest route. Sometimes we can be so pleased and relieved to have discovered a solution to our problem that we don't bother to look any further. But a little extra creative thought may well show that there are other possible – and perhaps preferable – solutions just around the corner. Remember that minds are like parachutes: they only work when they are open.

Logical thought

Nothing I have said is meant to suggest that logical left-brained thought is not valuable and, indeed, a vital part of the process of achievement. But it is not enough *on its own*. It has to form part of the whole. If the inventor of the wheel, all those centuries ago, had not combined creative thought with analytical thought, we would still be walking. The creative thought provided the concept while the logical thought gave him the way of turning that concept into reality.

In the same way, the artist contemplating the lump of cold, hard marble must first see, in his mind's eye, the beautiful statue he wishes to create. But this vision will be useless if he has not learned the techniques needed to use the tools and work the stone. Once again, the balance between left and right brain is needed to produce the finished article.

Imagination

Imagination is a vital component of creative thought. Without a lively imagination my student would never have come up with 113 uses for the knitting needle. Without imagination nothing new would ever be invented. The would-be inventor first has to imagine what he wants to create and then find a practical way of getting there. Once radio had been invented, it was probably easier to invent television because the inventor would have known what he wanted to achieve – a radio with pictures. Perhaps he said to himself: 'Wouldn't it be good if you could see the people on the radio as well as hear them?' Try using those words for yourself. A great deal of creative thought can come from 'Wouldn't it be good if . . . ?'

Visualisation

Visualisation involves the deliberate use of the imagination, and the ability to visualise what you want can often prove to be the first step in attaining it. It is such a vast and important topic when dealing with the acquisition of knowledge and the improvement of recall that you will find the whole of Chapter 5 is devoted to it.

Many famous people have used visualisation to help them solve their problems. Einstein, Edison and Galileo, among others, all explained how they would deliberately program their minds by picturing what it was they were attempting to achieve and then letting the brain's own computer do its work – often while they slept. You can try this for yourself. If you have a practical problem to solve, think about it when you go to bed at night. Don't try to find a solution, but simply feed in all the information and your requirements and then, as the saying goes, 'sleep on it'. In many instances you will find that you wake up either with the actual solution in your mind, or perhaps aware of the next step you must take.

The greater the part you allow imagination and visualisation to play in the learning process, the easier you will find both the acquiring of knowledge and the ability to recall it at will. It is much simpler to remember something you have seen in a picture than to recall an abstract principle. And if you can create a series of pictures rather than only one, so much the better.

When I was at school I was fortunate enough to have a history teacher who made the subject come alive by allowing us to act out the various events about which we had to learn. This necessitated thinking about the characters of the people we were portraying, why they acted as they did, and the results of their actions. Because we had temporarily 'become' those people with all their virtues and their faults, we were able to understand the events they precipitated and to recall them whenever we wished. In fact, not only did we all do well in our examinations, but I believe I could probably tell you now about what we learned in those history lessons – and they took place over thirty years ago!

My geography teacher, however, had a different set of ideas. She would give us seemingly endless lists of facts to learn by heart. Fascinating titbits of knowledge like the amount of rainfall in Karachi in the average October! (My apologies to the inhabitants of Karachi if they don't have any rain in October; the lists were so boring and meaningless that I never did remember them.)

It will not take you very long to decide which teacher used a more effective method. Suffice it to say that geography and I gave each other up at a very early stage.

Suppose, however, the geography teacher had gone about things differently. Suppose her pupils had been told that, because the climate in a particular place was of a certain type, the people could only grow certain crops, live in a particular kind of dwelling and lead a certain kind of life. Perhaps if those pupils had been asked to imagine what it must be like to live in that part of the world, given its geographical conditions, they would have enjoyed the subject and developed an interest in it for itself and not simply in order to pass the required examination.

Thought-flow charts

Thought-flow charts are a great aid to creative thinking, and they can help in all aspects of life from designing a five-year-plan for your business to making a packing list for the family holiday.

Thanks to our left-brained upbringing, almost all of us think in lists and this can be very limiting. A thought-flow chart does away with that self-imposed limitation. Suppose, for example, you were asked to write an essay or an article on gardening. You would naturally start by jotting down some of the points you would like to cover. Your list might begin like this:

1. Soil
2. Flowering plants
3. Pests
4. Lawn
5. Vegetables

The problem is that, by the time you come to write the word 'Vegetables' you have already forgotten all about item number one, 'Soil' – and this applies even more if you have numbered the items on your list. A thought-flow chart does just the opposite; it leaves every avenue open for further exploration.

Let's take that same essay or article on gardening. To make your own thought-flow chart, take a *large* sheet of paper (at least A4 size). In the centre write the word 'Gardening' and draw a circle around it. Now for every main topic you need to draw a line from that circle and write the word itself. In the example given here I have actually used the five items on our list above as the main topics. And if you look at the thought-flow chart shown here, you

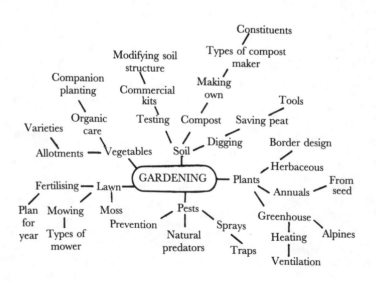

will see that each topic has given rise to several sub-topics. But, because of the shape and layout of the chart, no section is ever closed: you can go on adding more and more sub-topics until you run out of ideas (or paper). When your chart is completed you will find you have more than enough ideas for your essay or article. Indeed, each sub-topic could form the basis of an article in itself.

Becoming a more creative person

Another way in which you can help yourself to become a creative thinker is by trying to increase the creativity in the rest of your life. The changes you make may be relatively small ones but they will help you to develop a more creative attitude and, as your subconscious mind absorbs the nuances of change, you will find that your thought processes begin to change too.

Here are just a few suggestions for ways in which you can introduce more creativity into your daily routine:

1. Take up an artistic or creative hobby. You might decide to paint or draw, to make clay models, to arrange flowers, to sing or to play an instrument: there are so many pastimes from which you can choose. It does not matter if it is years since you did anything of this sort, or even if you think you have no talent. You are not setting out to thrill audiences in La Scala or to have an exhibition at the Royal Academy. The most important point is that the hobby you choose should be a source of pleasure to you and a complete contrast to your usual daily routine.

2. Allow yourself time to daydream. Set aside regular periods (perhaps in the bath?) during which you have nothing to do but indulge in flights of fancy. You could spend this time reliving happy memories of places you have seen or people you have known. Or you might think about your hopes for your own future or that of your children. Set these daydreams in motion by saying to yourself: 'Suppose . . .' or 'What if . . . ?'

3. Pay a little more attention to your night-time dreams. Like most people, you probably find it difficult to recall them once you are fully awake. Dreaming is governed by the right-hand side of the brain and is therefore naturally creative. And, if the dreamer is not actually at the centre of the 'plot', then his or her emotions are usually affected by what is taking place. I am not an expert on dream interpretation but it may well prove beneficial to keep a note of your dreams and see whether a pattern emerges which is trying to tell you something about yourself.

Few of us remember our dreams, but it is not difficult to learn to do so. These pointers may help you:

- Before going to bed, see that you have a pen and pad (or a cassette recorder if you prefer) on the table beside you.
- When you wake in the morning, get into the habit of lying still with your eyes shut and holding on to the last image of your dream. Now allow that image to led you to other, earlier ones. (When you start doing this, you may find that the final image is all you can recall. Don't let this worry you; the rest comes with practice).
- Make notes of what you have remembered by either writing them on your pad or recording them on an audio cassette. Do this before getting out of bed, as sudden physical activity seems to dispel the impressions you may retain of your dreams.

4. Try and find the time to read something which has nothing whatsoever to do with your work or studies. It does not matter whether you turn to science fiction, bodice-ripper romances or classical poetry. What is important is that it is a complete change from those books or periodicals you *have* to read.

5. Turn the pages of illustrated books or magazines depicting works of art or styles of interior design. Whether you actually like what you see is less important than the fact that you are training your mind to absorb a wide variety of shapes, designs and concepts.

6. Change your viewpoint – literally! Move the furniture so that you look at something different when you wake up in the morning or as you relax in your favourite armchair. In the office, turn your desk round so that you are facing in another direction. If practicalities, such as the dimensions of your room, make this impossible, vary the positions of the pictures on your walls or the ornaments on your shelves. You may decide that you preferred everything the way it was before (and there is nothing to stop you moving them back again after a while), but at least you will have tried to see things differently and you will have become conscious that there is always another perspective.

7. When you listen to music – whether you prefer Wagner or heavy metal – allow it to create images in your mind. Instead of letting the music form a backdrop of sound as you go about your daily routine, sit down, close your eyes and allow the sound to fill your thoughts. You may find that clear and detailed pictures come into your mind, or your head may be filled with abstract shapes and colours. Either way you will have tasted a whole new world of creativity.

8. Make a break with routine, or change your daily habits. Do you *always* travel to work by the same route? Does the family have a holiday by the sea *every* year? Do you *always* visit Aunt Maud on the Sunday after Easter? It is so easy to become set in a rut and to stifle much of your creative thought. If you make a change you may even open up a whole new world of experiences for yourself. A new route to work might provide you with some beautiful scenery or fascinating shops; a country holiday may turn out to suit you better than a crowded beach; if you visit her in the middle of winter, Aunt Maud may welcome you with a blazing log fire and crumpets for tea. Even something as simple as tuning to a different radio or television station can provide you with a new outlook as you hear other music played or opinions expressed.

9. If you have ever belonged to a debating society, you will know that you may sometimes be called upon to

argue a case from a viewpoint which is not really yours. Seeing things from another point of view – inverted thinking – is mind-stretching and creative. You may not have the time, desire or opportunity to join a debating society, but you can always play the debating game with friends or family. Decide upon a subject to discuss, then write the different standpoints on pieces of paper and put these in a bowl. Each person must then pick out a piece of paper and put forward the point of view written upon it – even if he is, in reality, diametrically opposed to it. The value of this game is that it helps you to see things from positions other than your own.

10. Try to add some spontaneity to your life. Do some things on the spur of the moment rather than only after careful planning. Naturally this cannot apply to all aspects of your existence, but I am sure you will find some areas where spontaneous action can introduce some fun and sparkle to a formerly mundane routine.

Relax

In Chapter 1 we looked at how relaxation can help your recall ability in specific situations. Relaxation can be beneficial in other ways too:

Planning

There is no point in trying to achieve too much too quickly: you will only succeed in stifling all creative thought. Start early and help yourself to have a relaxed attitude of mind by planning your study routine and deciding how much it is realistic for you to deal with at a time. In this way you will not be putting yourself under pressure, thereby causing tension, which makes learning a far more difficult process.

Brain waves

The brain has four principal frequencies: beta, alpha, theta and delta. The alpha state is the one which facilitates the rapid assimilation of facts and creates a heightened ability to recall. It is the right-brained state in which you daydream and in which your imagination is able to play its full role. It is also in the alpha state that you have flashes of inspiration. But unless you are relaxed, physically and mentally, it is not possible to enter the alpha state.

Attitude of mind

Accept the fact that, whatever your academic history, you *can* learn to learn. You have been learning things all your life. Just think of all that you are capable of doing. Whether it is walking, talking, changing a plug, speaking a foreign language, singing a song, boiling an egg or writing a thesis on differential calculus, it is something you have learned to do. Not only have you acquired the knowledge, you have retained it and recalled it when you wanted to. If this was not the case, every experience would seem like a new one – and, if you can remember things you have been doing for some time, there is no reason why you cannot learn to remember other skills too.

You can help yourself to develop your ability to think creatively if you allow relaxation to become part of your life. I don't mean the type of relaxation which simply means sitting down and doing nothing, although there is nothing wrong with that from time to time. But if you can acquire the habit of practising a relaxation technique for about ten or fifteen minutes a day, you will find it far easier to enter the alpha state and learning will cease to be a battle.

There are many ways of learning to relax. You may like to use the basic technique described in Chapter 5; you may prefer to attend a yoga or meditation class; you may decide to seek the outside help of a relaxation therapist, or to purchase a cassette. The way in which you learn is not important; it is the regular practice which can make all the difference to your life and your ability to learn.

3

Your Memory and How to Improve It

Everything said so far about the creative use of your mind begins to come alive when we start to look at memory and its function. Here, with practice, you can begin to take charge. It is not a case of 'I can remember' or 'I can't remember'; by combining creative thinking with the memory techniques described in this and other chapters, and relating it to what you already know, you can learn to assimilate knowledge more easily and to recall it at will.

Although we tend to speak of 'memory' and 'remembering' as though only one process was involved, there are actually two entirely separate stages:

- the ability to retain information in the first place, and
- the ability to recall it at will

Most of us are far better at retaining knowledge than we think – although our recall system often lets us down. This becomes apparent when we consider the evidence of people who, when placed under hypnosis, have been able to recall in great detail facts or events of which they had no conscious recollection. Provided either the details in question were naturally memorable (in a good or bad way) in themselves, or you have deliberately set about working at making them memorable, they will be lodged in your mind and available for recall at a later date.

Of course, many of the instances in which hypnosis is used to aid recall involve traumatic events which the conscious mind of the subject has deliberately quashed as a means of protection. But it is also true, for example, that if you were able to speak and understand another language as a small child but have forgotten it as you grew older, hypnosis can help you regain that former ability. Your fluency and comprehension, however, will be no greater than they were when that language played a part in your life. If your vocabulary then was limited to childish phrases, that is all you will be able to remember now.

Memory and age

It has long been thought that memory deteriorates as we grow older, but in fact this is far from the truth. There is more than enough room to store all the information you will ever need, and there will still be plenty of space left over. Think of your memory as a muscle. To stretch and expand the muscles in your arms, legs or body you take frequent and regular exercise. The more exercise you give your memory, the more flexible it will become and the more easily you will recall stored information. So do what you can to become more observant, to learn new words and to picture new images. Stretch your memory and it will continue to serve you well.

Perhaps one of the reasons for the belief that memory grows worse with age is that, with a far greater store of information built up over years of experience and acquired knowledge, the process of sifting and retrieving may take a little longer than before. It may also be that we become less observant or allow our concentration to wander, and therefore do not retain the information in the first place. Without retention there can be no recall, so the result is what we tend to call a 'poor memory'.

The three stages of memory

There are three different types of memory: immediate, short-term and long-term.

Immediate memory

Information stored in the immediate memory lasts for just a few seconds. Immediate memory exists to ensure that we do not forget why we went upstairs or opened the kitchen cupboard. But, having remembered the piece of information for long enough to act upon it, it is no longer needed and will be discarded by the mind as irrelevant.

Short-term memory

Although it is possible for facts to remain in the short-term memory for up to two years, a certain amount of repetition is necessary for this to happen. Because the short-term memory is easily distracted, we can, without that repetition, forget a fact within thirty seconds. (When you look up a number in the telephone directory you probably either write it down or repeat it over and over again, to keep it fixed in your memory until you have dialled it. Then you let it go. If the number turns out to be engaged so that you need to dial again, you will probably find that you have to look it up all over again.)

It is, however, possible at any time during the two-year period to transfer the information to the long-term memory. This is what happens with repeated study or revision.

Think of the way you react to popular songs. If a particular new song appeals to you, then, having heard it once or twice, it will be stored in the short-term memory. However, suppose that song becomes very popular and you hear it every time you turn on the radio or pass a record store (in other words it is regularly repeated – which is a form of automatic revision), that song will then pass into your long-term memory. Many years later, you will only have to hear the opening bars of the music to realise that you still know the tune and all the words.

Another example of short-term memory is the process of counting. Suppose, for example, you are counting the number of cards in a pack. Because you know that you will only need to remember each number for as long as it takes to reach the next one, you do not repeat it or try to transfer it to your long-term memory. But suppose you have just reached number 42 when someone comes into the room and interrupts your train of thought by asking you a question. This last number is likely to disappear from your memory, and you will have to go back to the beginning again.

It is really just as well, however, that things do fade from our short-term memory. If they did not, we would simply be storing up an inordinate amount of unnecessary clutter.

The short-term memory can hold up to about seven objects at any one time. More than seven and something will be lost (unless, of course, it is repeated and thereby transferred to the long-term memory). You can test this for yourself. Ask someone to read out a three-digit number and then see if you can repeat it. You will probably not have too much difficulty. Now do the same thing with a four-digit number, then five, then six, then seven. Unless this is an exercise you have practised over a period of time, it is doubtful whether you will be able to repeat a seven-digit number – and certainly not an eight-digit one (but see below for a way round the problem). Even if you turn out to be one of the few who can cope with a series of seven numbers, try again after one minute. Unless you have repeated the numbers to yourself, you will find that you are quite unable to remember them. And the same thing happens when you try to remember a series of seven or more letters.

It is possible to overcome this limitation to some extent by means of grouping. In other words, it would be almost impossible to remember the number 0716439258. Yet, if you happen to see those same digits written as a telephone number, that is, 071–643 9258, it would not seem so very difficult after all. Similarly, the word 'DIFFERENTIAL' has twelve letters, but it would be easy to remember because it forms a word. Trying to remember twelve random letters would be quite another matter. Provided the word is one you recognise, it is no harder to remember one containing twelve letters than one containing only four. So grouping certainly works.

Long-term memory

There is no limit to the amount of information you can keep in your long-term memory; so, unlike a store cupboard, you do not have to cast out old facts in order to make room for the new. And your long-term memory lasts for ever; anything stored there is capable of being retrieved at any time. In fact, when we use the word 'memory' it is really long-term memory we are referring to.

Think of your short-term memory as an in-tray, your long-term memory as a filing cabinet and a fact as a piece of paper. When the piece of paper reaches you, you have various options. You can glance at it, decide that it is of no interest to you whatsoever and throw it into the nearest waste-paper basket. You can place it in your in-tray or, if you know immediately that this particular piece of paper is important, you can file it at once, taking care to put it in the appropriate place in the filing cabinet to facilitate retrieval at will. Even if you put the paper in your in-tray you will at some point have to do something about it. You could act on it and then, having no further need of it, discard it (short-term memory). Or you could place it together with other relevant pieces of paper in your filing cabinet (long-term memory). But you have to do something with it. If you just leave it lying in the in-tray it will soon be covered up by other, more recent, pieces of paper – never to be seen again.

Each time you set about deliberately learning something, you are converting it from short-term to long-term memory. This conversion has three stages:

1. *Desire:* you must *want* to remember the relevant piece of information
2. *Repetition or review:* as when you repeat a name or telephone number until you have the chance to write it down
3. *Committal:* inserting the information into your mental filing system. This is achieved by associating it with what you already know, often using visualisation techniques (which will be more fully explained in Chapter 5).

How much can you remember?

How much you are able to remember is influenced by the following factors, some of which you can change and some of which you cannot.

1. *Your natural capacity:* this is something which cannot be changed, but it is so great that there is no need ever to try.
2. *Suppression:* this involves the deliberate blocking out of memory by the subconscious and is often an involuntary form of instinctive protection. It can be changed, but professional help is usually needed.
3. *The effect of education and upbringing:* this can be altered with practice and exercise, as this book sets out to prove. There are no barriers to your ability to learn unless you place them there. If those barriers were originally placed there by someone in your past and you allow them to remain, then you are allowing the past to win.
4. *Your motivation:* this is something you can change for yourself. Even if you are not particularly excited by certain pieces of learning you have to do, if they are necessary for you to achieve your goals, keep reminding yourself of the goals and your reasons for wanting to achieve them. Make yourself interested in what you have to study, and you will remember it. Just think of all those things you remember without any effort – the names of those you care for, and any facts which particularly interest you – and you will see that motivation plays a large part in memory.

Verbal and visual memory

These are the two principal aspects of deliberate memorisation. Of course, we all have involuntary memory too – when, for example, a particular aroma suddenly wafts us back to a specific time in the past.

Although we all use both verbal and visual memory to some degree, most people lean predominantly one way or the other. If you arrive at a supermarket only to discover that you have left the shopping list at home, do you remember the words you wrote on that list (verbal) or do you picture the items you need to buy (visual)?

Children who are still too young to speak and understand language have no option but to be visual in their remembering. It is not unusual for a child to have remembered an object in colour even though he or she may have been too young to know the word for the colour at that time.

Remembering visually is a right-brained activity, while verbal memory is left-brained. Neither is right or wrong but, since we have already decided that the ideal is to be as balanced as possible, perhaps you should try and develop whichever side comes less naturally to you.

As you read down the following list of words, place a tick by your method of calling them to mind, whether by means of logical understanding or the creation of a mental image.

Word	Verbal	Visual
lemon		
table		
garden		
Rolls Royce		
cat		
pillow		
sea		
book		
office block		
cake		
mother		
mountain		

If you find that you have an equal number of ticks, then you are reasonably left-/right-brain balanced. If there is a definite emphasis on one side or the other, try working on the weaker aspect.

To improve your visual memory, practise creating the appropriate images in your mind. Imagine you are going to be a police witness, and describe what the object looks like. To improve your verbal memory, pretend that you are a news reporter and write a logical description of it.

Increasing your interest and motivation

If you are to improve your memory, you must find a way of becoming more interested in whatever it is you wish to remember. Whatever your reason for learning and remembering, the desire must be there – whether you are involved in a course of study, need to pass exams, or want to remember birthdays of members of your family or facts with which you can impress your boss or your colleagues.

Concentrate not only on your immediate aims but also on your long-term ones. Why do you want to study a particular subject? What is the end result to be? The more aware you become of the reasons for what you are doing, the easier it will be to maintain a reasonable level of application and so achieve a higher rate of success.

In order to remember, it is necessary to be *involved*. Two students may attend evening classes in Italian conversation at a local adult education centre – but it is the one who is actually going to Italy on holiday next year who will find it easier to remember what he learns.

Think of the teenager classified as a 'poor learner' because he or she is unable to remember facts taught at school. In many cases that same teenager will have no difficulty whatsoever in remembering all the words of the songs of their pop idols. Another who is a keen football fan may find it impossible to remember historical facts and dates – and yet he will be able to list accurately names of team members and numbers of goals scored in football matches over a period of years. These, of course, are examples of natural interest. What you have to do is to find a way of making yourself interested in what you have to learn. Once you have discovered your motivation, keep reminding yourself of it and re-emphasising your interest to yourself.

Obtaining and understanding information

To retain something only in your short-term memory it may be sufficient to learn it by heart, without really taking in the meaning of the words you repeat to yourself. But if you are to be able to transfer any information to your long-term memory, you must fully understand that information in the first place.

Inaccuracy or lack of comprehension can cause many problems. It is not simply a case of making mistakes when retrieving wrongly stored facts. Since anything you learn in the future will have to be linked with what you are learning now, if there is an error in the latter, that error will be compounded many times over as you increase your store of information.

You must be able to make sense of what you wish to remember. It would be far easier, for example, to learn a list of words such as TRAIN, DOG, HOUSE and so on than to commit to memory a series of meaningless syllables like SPOL, HIMP and WOSK. Because the first words have specific meanings with which you are already familiar, you will automatically form a picture in your mind as you read them. Whereas you have nothing with which to link the words in the second list.

By linking new information with that already stored, you are increasing the size of the file in your long-term memory cabinet. Unlike card or paper files, these particular ones have a limitless capacity and can expand to absorb as much information as you wish to insert. In fact, it takes far less effort to insert new information into an existing file than it does to open a completely new one. Look at the new piece of information and ask yourself how it interrelates with what you know. If you are already familiar with a particular period of history, any fact which adds to that knowledge slots in easily. It would be much harder to find an appropriate niche for that fact if you knew very little about the era in question.

To be certain that you will remember something, you have not only to understand it but to be sure that you *really* know it in the first place. If you were asked today to describe (without looking) what is featured on the label of your favourite brand of jam or coffee, you might not be able to do so. This is not because you have not seen and handled a large number of these jars, but because you have never bothered to register precisely what is depicted on the label. It has never mattered to you and has never prevented you from reading the name and thereby recognising the brand. But perhaps this example will help you to see that committing something to memory involves several deliberate actions on your part.

Reinforcing

Once you are certain that you fully understand whatever it is that you wish to learn, you need to reinforce that understanding.

- You may choose to do this by the way in which you set out your notes, making use of page layout, coloured highlighter pens and so on
- You may decide to create a series of thought-flow charts so that your increased knowledge is set down in a logical order
- You may wish to make a list of essential key words which apply to the subject you are studying
- And, if the topic under consideration lends itself to the creation of visual images, you may wish to conjure some up. All these techniques can prove invaluable when you come to retrieve the information from the recesses of your memory at a later date.

Bear in mind in this context that you will recall most easily what you study at the beginning and end of each work period, plus anything which strikes you as outstanding. If something is not outstanding of itself, you can make it so by using coloured pens, dramatic layout or your own sense of the ridiculous when it comes to creating visual images.

Reviewing and rehearsing

However well you have understood the information, and however thorough the notes, diagrams and mental images you have created, it is essential to review the material several times if you are to fix it permanently in your long-term memory. The intervals between reviews should lengthen, the ideal time-spans between them being:

First review: shortly after the initial learning period (perhaps after a rest of five or ten minutes)
Second review: the following day
Third review: one week later
Fourth review: one month later
Fifth review: three months later

If you follow the recommended review pattern, you will find that, when the time for an examination approaches, a careful reading of your notes should be enough to bring all the facts to the forefront of your mind once again.

When you review or rehearse what you have been studying, be selective about the information you choose. There is no point in trying to remember every single word; it is quite sufficient to rehearse the key facts. If these are fixed in your mind, you will be quite capable of turning them into fluent language.

Repeated reviewing of a subject is not only an effective method of transferring information from short- to long-term memory. It also makes further learning easier, as you will have an enlarged background knowledge into which to incorporate additional facts.

Recall

Recall is the ability to retrieve the information you have stored in your long-term memory filing cabinet. As with office filing cabinets containing pieces of paper, the more methodical the original system of storage, the easier it will be to find what you want when you want it.

Recall falls into two categories: deliberate and involuntary. Involuntary recall takes place when you instantly recognise an old friend you happen to meet in the street, or when you are watching a film you have seen before and know in advance what the ending will be. Deliberate recall occurs when you make an effort to remember something, in an exam, for example. Consider the following:

1. Think of a picture or ornament you have in your home – something you see almost every day. You know it is there; you recognise it every time you see it. This is involuntary recall. Deliberate recall would involve either making a precise drawing of the object, or describing it in fine detail. This, of course, is far more difficult.

2. If you are someone who reads widely, you will have little trouble recognising even those words with difficult or seemingly illogical spelling: this is involuntary recall. But will you do as well if asked to use your powers of deliberate recall to spell those words without having them in front of you?

These examples show that deliberate recall, which involves effort and concentration on your part at the stage of input, is, perhaps not surprisingly, more difficult than involuntary recall.

Some people find deliberate recall hard, and may be tempted to give up and say they 'don't know' or 'can't remember'. And yet it often takes just a slight hint to bring the piece of information to the forefront of their mind.

Suppose, for example, you were asked to name the four fairies in Shakespeare's *A Midsummer Night's Dream*. Even if you knew their names at some stage, you might find this difficult, particularly if you had not seen or read the play for some time. But, as any crossword fanatic will tell you, just a single letter can help you to remember what you thought you had forgotten. Try:

P – – – – – – – – – –

C – – – – –

M – – –

M – – – – – – – – –

and see if that helps. If you were still uncertain (and provided, of course, you knew their names in the first place) a multiple-choice answer might clarify the situation. You could probably say which of these were the right names:

Dandini	Tinkerbell
Cobweb	Moth
Bluebell	Ariadne
Petal	Mustardseed
Peaseblossom	Pansy
Daisy	Phoebe

Similarly, if someone is asked: 'Who wrote *A Tale of Two Cities*?' they will be either able or unable to invoke deliberate recall and give the answer. Yet, if they ever knew the name of the author, being given a choice (1. Shaw 2. Shakespeare 3. Dickens 4. Galsworthy) might 'ring a bell' – which is another way of saying, 'bring into play their involuntary recall ability'.

To ensure a strong ability to recall essential information deliberately, you have to concentrate particularly on the reviewing and revising aspect of learning. Without this repeated revision, even those facts in the long-term memory are going to slip to the back of the file and be more difficult to retrieve. That is the bad news. The good news is that any information you have learned correctly (however long ago) can be relearned with far less effort than information which is new to you.

Suppose, for example, you learned to speak French many years ago but you have not used the language for some time. If someone asks you to 'speak French' you might find it extremely difficult. But you would probably only need to spend a day or two in France to find all that old knowledge returning.

Making it easier to commit to memory

Because we are all different, methods which appeal to one person will not necessarily be suitable for another. But all the hints and methods below are effective ways of transferring information from your short-term to your long-term memory. Test them all for yourself and see which are the most helpful to you.

- Use the analogy of painting a window frame or a wall. First you use a primer, then an undercoat and then one or more topcoats to achieve the finish you desire. Remembering is very similar. Only add a new layer when you are completely happy with the one beneath.
- Take frequent breaks during your study time. Remember that we are all best able to recall what we learned at the beginning and end of each session. So give yourself several short sessions, and you will automatically remember more with less effort.
- Sequences are particularly helpful in the initial stages of learning. After all, when we are very young and learning to count or to recite the days of the week, we do not start off with '1, 4, 6, 2, 5, 3 . . .' or 'Wednesday, Monday, Saturday'. We learn them in their correct order. Once we become really familiar with them, we do not have to chant the whole list to know that Thursday comes after Wednesday or that 4 lies between 3 and 5.

  Always try and see a logical pattern in facts as they are presented to you. If you are studying history, a pattern will exist naturally; a play or novel will have its own innate sequence; a chemical experiment will follow a logical progression. If you are studying from a book or as part of a course, the compiler will already have thought out the pattern for you. Learning – and later recall – will come much more easily if you are aware of the underlying pattern. If you are not happy with the sequence of thought presented to you, spend a little time creating your own. And if you are writing your own notes or compiling a presentation, make sure that your facts flow naturally from one another. It will be simpler for you to learn and recall and also be more readily understandable to other people.
- Group together pieces of information you wish to remember. It is less difficult to recall a group than a series of isolated words, dates or facts. If grouping is not some-

thing you do naturally, you may like to try the following exercises:

Look around the room and group the items in it. You may choose to do this literally (the table is next to the chair in front of the window); you may do it by colour (the curtains, the cushions and the flowers in the vase are all pink) or by texture (the window, the coffee table and the television screen are all smooth). See how many different methods you can think of.

Below is a list of words. How would you group them?

apple	book
Christmas tree	daffodil
dog	coin
umbrella	aeroplane
old lady	cowboy

By the way, there is no right or wrong answer to this. It is up to you to group the words in any way you wish. You might choose to link the obvious and say that some of them are people, some are things which grow and so on. Or you could use your imagination and invent a little story – an old lady with an umbrella taking a dog for a walk in a field of daffodils, or a cowboy handing over a coin in exchange for an apple and a book.

- It often helps both comprehension and retention if you speak the facts aloud to yourself. Pretend you are giving as detailed an explanation as possible to someone who knows nothing about a subject. This is an excellent way of highlighting any gaps in your knowledge.

- If possible, find a friendly colleague or family member who is willing to test you on what you have learned. By giving an explanation in your own words to someone else, you will prove that you are completely familiar with what you have been studying.

- Isolated facts are very difficult to remember. Always try and combine new information with existing knowledge.

- Take charge of your own mental filing process. *Choose* the file into which you are going to insert your new piece of information. Of course, in life it is not always possible to know precisely what is going to be important in the future – but you can usually make an educated guess. If you are involved in a course of study, it is a good idea to relegate information which is not immediately relevant to a lower priority file. Be like Scarlett O'Hara in *Gone with the Wind* and 'think about it tomorrow'.

- Make use of technology. Record relevant data on to an audio cassette and play it all the time – when washing, cleaning the car, cooking and so on. Provided you have understood the information in the first place, this is a very effective way of fixing the facts in your long-term memory file and it works particularly well with such things as foreign language vocabulary and lists of dates. In these days of personal cassette players with earphones you do not even have to drive all those around you to distraction, as was formerly the case.

- The more ordinary or mundane the way in which a fact is presented, the more difficult it is to remember. The more outstanding, funny or peculiar it is, the more readily you will recall it. The more laughable the pictures you create in your mind, the easier they will be to re-create at will. It is also the reason for using coloured highlighter pens in your notes – you are literally making the information stand out from the ordinary.

- If you have a strong visual memory, or if you are working to develop it, try and remember the shapes created in your notes by the series of headings and sub-headings you will find described in Chapter 8. Calling to mind this layout will help to establish a pattern in your mind, and this in turn will make it easier to learn and remember. Use thought-flow charts to test your memory. Start by putting the central theme or title in the circle in the middle of the page. If you follow a logical progression of thought and have understood what you have been studying, you should be able to fill in the details.

- It is possible for anyone (other than some of those who suffer from particular diseases affecting the brain) to improve their memory, provided they are willing to put in the time and effort. There are 'memory tricks' such as the peg-word system (detailed in Chapter 5) which can amaze onlookers. Although these are not really part of the learning process, they should not be decried as they do serve as an exercise to help stretch the memory.

- Mnemonics can be helpful and do not stop at the colours of the rainbow. Many of those who are learning how to read music remember 'Every Good Boy Deserves Friends' to remind them that the five lines are E G B D F; similarly the spaces are F A C E – represented by the word 'face'. Did you ever learn, as I did, that the word 'HOMES' represents the five great lakes in North America – Huron, Ontario, Michigan, Erie and Superior? I am certain that you are well able to invent mnemonics of your own to help you with your particular subject.

- Use rhythm and rhyme as a memory aid. Even a small child who does not understand the full meaning of the words is able to sing a nursery rhyme. I still recall the rhyme at the front of my history book in school (*many* years ago) which listed the kings and queens of England. It began:

> Willy, Willy, Harry, Ste,
> Harry, Dick, John, Harry Three

(in other words William I, William II, Henry I, Stephen, Henry II, Richard, John, Henry III). Now, because it was never necessary for me to spend much time studying that particular period of history, I am positive I would not remember the order of those early monarchs had it not been for the rhyme. The writers of radio jingles and television commercials – who, after all, are very anxious for their creations to be memorable – usually concentrate on basic rhythm or rhymes to achieve this end. The Eurovision Song Contest is usually criticised for the relative inanity of its competing songs but, if they wish to appeal to judges who may not be able to understand what the contestants are singing about, the composers have little choice but to stick to fairly basic rhythms and tunes.

- Use chanting as a memory aid. Chanting is used, for instance, when young children are learning to recite their tables or how to spell some of the longer words. For example: 'With a D, with an I, with an F, F, I, with a C, with a U, with an L, T, Y.' Experiment and see whether you are one of those people who find chanting helpful when learning such things as lists.

4
Seeing and Observing

There is a vast difference between what we see (or *subconsciously* observe) and what we *consciously* observe. If you walked down the street this morning you probably *saw* the faces of dozens of other people. How many of them do you actually remember well enough to be able to describe? Yet, if you had not seen them, and they had not seen you, there would have been nothing to prevent you from bumping into each other. Similarly, there must have been any number of trees or lamp-posts (depending upon whether you were walking in town or country). I am assuming that, since you are well enough to be reading this book, you did not bump into those either. So you must have *seen* them. But can you recall just how many of each you passed and precisely where they were? I doubt it, even if you were walking along a familiar street.

Suppose, however, one of the women walking along that street had been wearing an outrageous, brightly coloured outfit: you would remember that. Or perhaps, hanging from one of the lamp-posts, was a large poster advertising some event which interested you: you would remember that. Why should that be? Simply because those two sights would have caught your attention sufficiently for you to *concentrate* upon them long enough to fix them in your memory. *Conscious observation* only arises from *concentration*.

Of course, *subconscious* observation is fine for the mundane areas of our everyday life. How boring it would be if the only way we could avoid walking into lamp-posts was to concentrate seriously on each one. But if you wish to set about the deliberate acquisition of new knowledge, then conscious observation is essential.

Let's look at some more examples:

You might know that (at the time of writing) the British £10 note is brown in colour; you might know that it bears a picture of Her Majesty the Queen on the front. Do you know who is pictured on the reverse of that note? And yet you have probably seen and handled one on numerous occasions. If you have a £10 note available, have a look at it.

Some of you will probably be feeling rather pleased with yourselves because you knew that the picture on the reverse shows Florence Nightingale. But before you grow too smug – and without looking at the note again – can you answer these two questions:

- Florence Nightingale is shown on the right of the note; what scene is depicted on the left?
- The dates of Florence Nightingale's birth and death are given in the bottom right-hand corner of the note; what are they?

Now you have just looked at the note, and you even saw the picture of the lady herself; there is nothing wrong with your eyesight. And yet I doubt if many of you have answered those two questions correctly. You must have seen the whole of the note when you looked at it but you only concentrated on – and therefore only observed – the part I had asked you about.

Acknowledging the fact that it is not possible to remember something without first observing it, the later recollection will be much simpler if what you see can be linked with something you already know. It will be far easier to remember that the picture on the reverse of the £10 note is that of Florence Nightingale if you have already heard of her. A strange name taken at random would soon pass from your memory unless you were able to find something in your mind to which you could link it.

This linking of what we see and what we know is essential to accurate recall. We have all seen rainbows in the sky but most of us, if asked to recite the sequence of colours, will still go back to the little phrase we learned as children: *R*obert *O*f *Y*ork *G*ave *B*attle *I*n *V*ain – *R*ed, *O*range, *Y*ellow, *G*reen, *B*lue, *I*ndigo, *V*iolet.

- Inventing such ciphers and codes to help root in our minds a visual image – or indeed any piece of random information – can be both amusing and beneficial.

A fashion designer with whom I am acquainted invented a code of her own for use at the French and Italian couture shows where you are not allowed to make drawings or take photographs of the latest creations of the top designers. She would have different letters for the various types of cut, drape, length and so on and would concoct little phrases to fix the designs in her mind until she could get to her drawing board.

Most of us have a tendency to see what we expect to see and to read what we expect to read. Ask any author who has carefully perused the final proofs of a book before publication whether any spelling or printing errors have still managed to slip through the net. Because we know what is *supposed* to be there, that is what we see. Try this test on your friends. Read the following phrase aloud exactly as it is written: 'The band was playing those old familar songs we love to hear'. With very few exceptions, if any, everyone will say the word 'familiar' when reading that phrase – and yet I have deliberately written 'familar'. Even if you asked them to read it exactly as written, they are unlikely to have noticed that the word had a missing letter. They will have seen what they expected to see.

Here's another example. Select any room in your home and imagine that every item in it has disappeared and you have to fill in an insurance claim form. Take your time and (without going into the room to look) list *every single item* in that room. I think you will be surprised, when you go and check, to see how many things you have missed. And yet you knew they were there, didn't you? You may even have placed them there yourself. And what is more, you may have been looking at them for days, weeks, months or even years.

Of course, had someone asked you a direct question (What is on the table by the window? How many cushions are on the sofa?) you would probably have been able to answer it quite easily. So in this case it is not your initial observation which is defective, but your ability to recall what you have observed. This, however, is something you can improve with practice.

We all observe far more than we realise, but this observation may be made subconsciously. Hypnotherapists are able to help their patients remember happenings they have long forgotten – and even facts, people and events they did not realise they knew. If you are to make use of your power of recall in order to assist you in the learning process, you need to develop your ability to observe *consciously*. The following exercises will help you:

- Think of someone you know quite well. How would you describe them so that they sounded different to anyone else and could be easily recognised by someone who had never before met them? It is much harder than you might think. Mary may be slim with short, brown hair and blue eyes, but so are thousands of others. If you cannot find a way to make her unique, perhaps you should look more closely at her next time you meet.

  Anyone who has been present in court when bystanders have attempted to explain what happened at the scene of an accident will know only too well that there will be as many different descriptions of the event as there are witnesses, even when none of the people concerned was personally involved in any way and each is endeavouring to give a true and honest account. Not only will descriptions of individuals vary but so will details of time, sequence, weather and so on. None of these people was waiting for the accident to happen, so none of them was concentrating on the scene. When it did take place, what they saw becomes associated in their minds with what their logic tells them must have happened, until eventually they are unable to separate observation from thought and the two combine to form an erroneous memory.

- Do you remember the game often played at children's parties, where a selection of items are placed on a tray and everyone looks at them for several minutes before the tray is covered with a cloth and contestants have to write down as many of the items as they can recall? You could practise this on your own at home – not as a competition, but as an observation-stretching exercise. The trick is to *look* at the items themselves, the pattern they make and their relationship to each other, rather than simply try and make a mental list of them. As you become more proficient at this exercise, you can make it harder for yourself by adding more and more items to the tray.

- If you are in a public place or on a long journey, select a nearby stranger and imagine you are going to have to describe him (or her) and his actions to the police. Look at the face, the stance, the clothes, the movements; what could you say about them which would make them easy to identify? (It is not a good idea to let your 'suspect' catch you doing this. At best it could cause embarrassment; at worst he or she might take offence and confront you!)

Observation involves interest in the subject at which you are looking. If you cannot arouse any interest, you will not concentrate. If you do not concentrate, then you will not observe. And without observation there can be no recall. If you are treading warily, trying to keep your balance on an icy path, you do not notice the people passing by. If you are deeply in love and devoting all your attention to one person, you may not hear or see what is going on around you.

It also works the other way around. You may have no interest at all in cars but, as soon as you buy one of a particular make, you seem to see similar models everywhere you go. Your interest in your own vehicle and its selection has made you observe features about it which you would otherwise not have realised existed. It is these features which you are then able to recognise instantly, even in a car which is speeding past you in the opposite direction.

Observation is linked not only to sight but to other senses too. Many people, if distressed or engrossed in what they are reading, are capable of eating a meal which has been placed before them without either tasting it or being able to tell you what it was.

We also cease to observe what is around us all the time. We may see – and hear – the traffic outside the office window, but we are not conscious that we have done so and we do not observe it. It is something which is present every single day and therefore becomes like 'mental wallpaper' – when was the last time you actually *looked at* the paper on your walls? Go into any factory where there is a constant hum of machinery and you may wonder how anyone could bear to work there; the answer is that those who do have lived with the sound for so long that they are no longer aware of it.

The human brain is only capable of maintaining one thought at a time. So, if we are to observe and to recall, we need to concentrate upon whatever we are looking at. Otherwise it will not make a strong enough impression. I am sure you know people who will tell you that they can read a book and listen to the radio at the same time. What happens in reality is that their attention keeps flitting from one to the other. If the reading and the radio programme are both fairly light, this may be all that is needed to grasp the gist of what is happening. But, if you need to remember whatever it is that you are reading, you must concentrate on it to the exclusion of all else. There is no harm in a little background music, but you will not be able to learn effectively if both the sounds and the reading matter are vying for your attention.

There are several stages to improving your powers of concentration:

1. If you have something you need to do, do it before settling down to your studies. If you don't, it will only niggle at you and cause your attention to wander.
2. Learn to relax. The more tense you are, the more difficult you will find it to concentrate. So get into the habit of practising a relaxation routine before starting a period of study.
3. Practise. No skill worth having comes without practice. In this case, you need to start by practising little and often and gradually increase the length and complexity of your task. Begin with a short passage of simple text. It

is better by far to set yourself a small goal and achieve it than to aim for a mammoth one and fail miserably.

4. Develop an interest in your subject. Sometimes this is easy because some topics will naturally intrigue you. But it is frequently the case that we have to study a particular subject we find boring simply in order to obtain a qualification. If that applies to you, try and make the end result the point of interest – whether it is the qualification itself, or the position it will enable you to obtain, or the money you hope to earn.

5. Always try to link new facts or ideas to what you already know. Learning words 'parrot fashion' may help you to pass an examination tomorrow, but the knowledge will never stick and all the effort will have been to no avail.

6. Pictures are far easier to remember than words – think of the advertising industry and how they bombard us with pictures in order to keep their products firmly fixed in our minds. If you are able to turn what you learn into mental images, it is far more likely to remain in your mind and be easier to recall. You can practise this for yourself. When you read a newspaper item which is not already illustrated, conjure up a mental picture to look at.

5
The Value of Visualisation

You already have in your possession one of the most valuable aids to learning – your own imagination. Your imagination and the way in which you use it can be of inestimable value when it comes to studying, memorising and preparing for test situations (whether the taking of formal examinations or the moment when you have to stand before an audience and give a presentation or make a speech).

What is visualisation?

Visualisation is the ability to harness the power of your imagination and create pictures in your mind which are relevant to the task you have in hand.

You may be thinking that you are one of those people who does not have the ability to create images inside your head, and yet this is something which can be achieved by anyone – with the exception of those who have had the misfortune to be blind from birth and who, therefore, have no point of reference from which to begin. Anyone who has – or has ever had – the ability to see is capable of creating pictures in their own imagination. All of us are born with the ability to visualise clearly but sometimes, often as a result of an extremely left-brained upbringing and education, this ability diminishes through lack of use. But even if you have temporarily lost this valuable tool, you can regain it in a comparatively short time and, having regained it, can use it to help in any learning process, whether you are engaged in full-time study, working towards promotion or professional exams or catching up on new systems which have been introduced while you were away from the work-place.

Not only will increasing your ability to visualise help you in the particular ways I shall go on to describe, but it will also help you to develop your ability to use your right brain. As we saw earlier, a good balance between left and right brain is essential if we are to become adept at learning.

Improving your ability to visualise

Suppose you are one of those people whose visual imagination has been allowed to fall into disuse. How are you going to set about strengthening it? It is really not as difficult as you might think and, if you will just follow the sequence of simple exercises detailed below, you will soon find that you can create vivid and exciting mental pictures.

1. Take any simple household object – a jug, a teapot or a vase, for example. Place it on the table and sit facing it. Really look at the object you have chosen; don't simply think to yourself: 'That is a vase' or even: 'That is a large vase.' Take in its shape, its colour, the way the handle is joined to the main body, the way the lip is formed, whether it is white or coloured, whether it is patterned or plain. When you think you know that vase quite well, close your eyes and try to form a picture of it in your mind. (You may find this quite difficult at first, particularly if you have been out of the habit of using your imagination for a long time.)

   This is a mind-stretching exercise and not a test: you cannot 'pass' or 'fail'. So, if you do find it difficult to picture the jug in your mind, open your eyes and have another look at it. Do this as often as is necessary for you to be able to close your eyes and picture the jug whenever you want.

   Practise this exercise every day until you are able to perform it with no trouble at all.

2. Sit quietly in a place of your choosing – perhaps in a park, a garden or a library. Look around you at all those

things you tend to take for granted. Look at the shape of the place and at each thing you can see from where you are sitting. Take note of the relative sizes and positions of different items and the effects of light and shade. Look at textures and colours. Think about the atmosphere: how does this place make you *feel*? When you have done all that, close your eyes and try to reconstruct the view in your imagination, remembering to visualise it rather than to tell yourself what you know is there. If you have any difficulty, simply open your eyes for a moment to refresh your memory.

This exercise too should be practised daily until you find it easy.

3. Now go through a similar process but without first giving yourself the opportunity to study what you are going to visualise. Try to picture the view from a window in your home. You may be surprised to find how difficult this exercise can be, even if it is a view you see every day of your life. Spend some time on this exercise before going to check and see how accurate you are. Repeat it every day (perhaps using various windows and views) until you are able to do it with ease.

4. The final exercise involves visualising something which you cannot check for confirmation – an image from your past. Choose any time you like in your past, whether it was last week or twenty years ago. Begin with the most outstanding part of that memory and allow the rest gently to unfold in your imagination. Although you will not be able to prove to yourself whether or not you have remembered correctly, your visualisation ability should have developed sufficiently by now for you to create vivid images in your mind.

The uses of visualisation

Creative visualisation has many beneficial uses, ranging from improving your health to developing self-awareness from your dreams, and I have attempted to deal with these fully in my book *Elements of Visualisation*. Within the scope of learning to learn there are also many ways in which this employment of the imagination can be valuable. These include:

- Aiding relaxation
- Transferring information to your long-term memory
- Assisting recall and retrieval
- Conquering exam nerves
- Remembering names and faces
- Remembering lists and random items

Aiding relaxation

You may be wondering why I have put relaxation at the top of the list of uses of visualisation, but in many instances it is a valuable – if not an essential – first step. The more relaxed you are when you set about learning, the easier it is to transfer information from your short-term to your long-term memory. The more relaxed you are, the more readily you will conquer those examination or performance nerves which beset most of us. And of course, as we saw earlier, the more relaxed you are the more oxygen will flow to your brain, enabling you to remain alert, and to think both quickly and effectively.

Relaxation is a deliberate process and not, as so many people think, just flopping down in front of the television set and doing nothing. If you can make the commitment to spend ten minutes every day practising true relaxation, you will notice a real change in yourself after a comparatively short period of time. You will be less tense and less anxious and you will have an increased sense of physical well-being. All this for just ten minutes of your time each day!

The breathing exercise given on p. 68 is one of the elements of relaxation – but only one. You also need to relax your muscles and your mind. Some experts might suggest that you try to 'make your mind blank' but, unless you have been practising one of the more advanced forms of yoga or meditation for some time, you are unlikely to be able to achieve this. And the frustration you feel at your failure is quite likely to induce more tension rather than less. This is where visualisation comes in. If you are not going to make your mind blank, you certainly do not want it to be filled with all the everyday niggles and worries plus any problems you may be experiencing in relation to your studies. The solution is to fill your mind with something else so that there is no room for any of those anxieties to find a hold.

There are many ways of inducing a sense of true relaxation. Whatever method you choose, the basic components do not change. A step-by-step method for you to follow is given below. Once you have been practising for a while you may decide to change the process a little to suit your own personal preferences, but this method is certainly one which is effective and so it will make a good starting-point.

1. Choose a time when you are unlikely to be disturbed and when you are not anxiously watching the clock because you have an appointment. Unplug the telephone if there is no one else there to answer it.

2. Sit or lie comfortably. You may choose to lie on the floor or on your bed or you may prefer to sit in a chair. The important thing is to feel comfortable. To do this you will need to have your head and neck supported, so if you are in a chair make sure its back is high enough to do this.

3. See that none of your clothing is tight or restrictive. Then close your eyes and start to breathe slowly and regularly. Do this for a few minutes.

4. If a muscle is to be really relaxed, you first of all have to tense it. So, starting from your feet and working upwards through your body, tense and relax each set of muscles in turn. Pay particular attention to those of the head, jaw, neck and shoulders, as this is where the greatest tension is usually experienced.

5. Starting from your feet once again, work through each set of muscles and, using your imagination, become conscious of how heavy they are growing.

6. Once you have completed these sequences, it is time to use your powers of visualisation. Instead of trying to empty your mind, simply imagine a scene which you would find beautiful. For one person this will be a leafy

glade; for another a snowy mountainside; for yet another a tropical seascape. It is up to each individual to choose the picture which most pleases them. The place you visualise may be real, or you may prefer to create one in your imagination. As long as you find it beautiful and peaceful, it does not matter.

7. Remain in your chosen beauty spot for several minutes – and enjoy the experience. Look at it from all angles and get to know it well. Absorb the atmosphere of the place you have imagined: how does it make you *feel*? When you feel ready to do so, simply open your eyes and sit or lie quietly for a few moments.

Transferring information to your long-term memory

There are several ways in which visualisation can help you to transfer information from the short-term to the long-term memory. You may find that one method suits you better than another, but do give each one a fair chance by trying it over a period of time. In fact, if you are to become a well-balanced left- and right-brained individual, it is those methods which do not come naturally to you which you should practise most often.

It is a frequently quoted statistic in business circles that words, whether spoken or read, only account for a minor proportion of information given and received. The precise percentage varies according to the source of reference, but it is generally accepted as being less than 20 per cent. The other 80 or so per cent comes from illustrations, whether actual (perhaps diagrams, graphs or slides) or conceived (in the imagination of the recipient). So work on your own creative visualisation ability by testing the techniques given below:

1. Translate what you hear or what you read into 'mind movies' and watch them unfold inside your head. However much you have enjoyed a book, it is often far easier to recall a story if you have seen the film, or the play, too. So, whatever the subject you are studying, give yourself time to visualise what you have learned.

Suppose, for example, you are studying a set of statistics about the business in which you are (or hope to be) involved. All too often the tendency is to attempt to sit down and learn the relevant facts and figures by heart. Apart from the fact that this a boring task and you are therefore more likely to give up at an early stage, even if you commit an entire list to memory you may well become flummoxed when asked to deal with one statistic in particular.

Now suppose that you take the same statistics and, having spent a few moments practising your relaxation technique in order to allow the images to penetrate your subconscious more easily, you translate those statistics into appropriate images. You might help the process along by asking your self such questions as:

- What do these statistics tell me about the business with which I am concerned?
- Do they encourage an optimistic or pessimistic view of the future?
- What will be the effect on the working life of the people employed in the business?
- What will be the knock-on effect on their home and family life?
- What new systems or ideas can be introduced into the business and what will be their effects?
- What part would I choose to play in such changes?

I am sure you can think of many more such questions for yourself. In answering them you will be able to create a mental image of the organisation concerned and the outlook for it and the people who work within it. The statistics will be mere figures no longer, and therefore far more readily recalled.

2. Bear in mind that anything outstanding or ridiculous is much easier to remember, so use your creativity to form amusing pictures in your mind.

If you have to learn about a particular historical character, it does not matter at all if you have no idea what he or she really looked like. Invent an image for yourself and become familiar with it. Now let us suppose that your historical character performed some notable act in the year 1674 and that this is a date you need to remember. Why not give him the most up-to-date digital wristwatch to wear – one which shows the year as well as the time? I know and you know that such watches did not exist in 1674 but, if you see your famous person checking the date by pressing the button on this ultra-modern piece of technology, you are far more likely to recall the date itself. Or perhaps he has a dramatic, memorable (or even rude) calendar hanging on the wall showing the relevant date. Use your own imagination to develop this idea to incorporate any other facts you need to remember.

Think of the stories you remember without any effort at all, and you will realise that this method works. Unless you are an avid and regular reader of the Bible, you may not know a great deal about Elisha or Boaz, but I am sure you recall the main features of the stories of Jonah, of David and Goliath, or of Samson and Delilah. Why is this? Probably because, like me, you created your own image as a child of Jonah sitting, fully clothed, inside the body of the whale while he waited patiently for the great creature to open its jaws so that he might escape. Or you imagined Delilah cutting the locks from Samson's head with a pair of scissors.

3. Having written your notes and established the key words of what you have to learn, try the following: close your eyes and relax by your chosen method. Now see in your imagination those words being written by some unseen giant hand. There are several important points about this technique:

- The writing must be done very slowly, one letter at a time.
- Each word should be written in capital letters as this causes it to be imprinted even more firmly on your subconscious.
- There must be a stark contrast between the words and the material on which they are written, so you could choose either black writing on white paper or white chalk on a blackboard.

- Do not try to work on too many key words at one time. A maximum of five is advisable.
- At this stage you are not being tested. If you reach word three and then find you cannot go on, simply open your eyes and look at the next word. If you put yourself under pressure by thinking of it as a test exercise, you will find that you do not retain the information for so long a period.

  Do not progress to the next set of key words until you have been able successfully to repeat the first set at least three times.

4. If you have already written your notes using highlighter pens and underlining headings and sub-headings (see Chapter 8), you will find that a pattern has emerged on the page. Try to visualise that pattern, or even to relate it to the image of an object, and you will find the wording of the headings and so on far easier to recall.

Assisting recall and retrieval

If you have been using visualisation to help you absorb facts in the first place, you will find that the recall process becomes far less arduous.

Let's go back to our 1674 character. If you have been able to create a picture of him in your mind and have allowed yourself to become familiar with it, the mere mention of his name will be sufficient to cause you to re-create that mental image – just as you have an instant picture in your mind when you hear someone refer to a close friend or relative.

Once you can visualise the person concerned, all other images will follow. So you will see his watch or his calendar bearing the relevant date. And you will be able to watch his exploits as if on a film in your mind.

If you have chosen to commit key words to memory by visualising them being written slowly on that imaginary board or piece of paper, reference to any one of those words will enable you automatically to re-create the entire list.

Of course, all this depends upon you having understood the information at the outset – but, had you not done so, you would not have been able to convert the facts into those visual images in the first place.

Conquering exam nerves

No matter how hard you have studied and how well you think you know your subject, it is perfectly natural to be a little apprehensive when exam time comes around. This natural apprehension will do you no real harm, and may even be beneficial as the extra adrenalin produced will help you to think on your feet and to give a good performance.

Problems arise, however, when that natural anxiety is replaced by blind panic. We have all met excellent students who do themselves scant justice when taking examinations because they allow excessive nervousness and agitation to render them incapable of clear and lucid thought. It has even been known for students who have worked thoroughly and competently during the term to fall so great a victim to panic that they have been unable to write a single word on the exam paper. Even putting aside such extreme cases, more people fail examinations through nervousness and anxiety than through lack of knowledge and preparation.

Perhaps because of the high incidence of extreme tension at exam time, most schools and colleges now take into account much of the year's work when arriving at final marks. This continuous assessment, however, will never completely eliminate the need for tests and examinations. Perhaps this is no bad thing, as life itself is always going to confront you with test situations or times when you will be put on the spot in the same way as you are when sitting an exam.

The technique I am going to explain will help to overcome extremes of nervousness and enable you to perform at your best. But don't make the mistake of thinking that you will get away with doing any less preparatory work; nothing is going to take the place of careful and continuous learning. The aim here is to assist you in demonstrating that knowledge by allowing you to think clearly and calmly when confronted with a test paper or an oral examiner.

For this method to work well, you really need to begin using it about three weeks before the exam so that your subconscious mind has time to forge a permanent link between the thought of the exam and the sensation of serenity. Set aside a specific time each day for this exercise, which need take no more than fifteen minutes or so. An ideal time to practise it is in bed at night just before going to sleep, as this also allows your subconscious to work on it without distraction during the whole of the night.

1. Begin by going through the early stages of the relaxation technique already described (see p. 68). Tense and relax each set of muscles, breathe slowly and regularly, and imagine your body growing progressively heavier.

2. Now picture yourself in the exam situation. Even if you are not familiar with where it is to take place, the format is almost identical in every case. You will sit at a desk or table with other students around you; there will be silence and, at a given moment, you will turn over the exam paper and begin. See the whole scene in your imagination, reminding yourself all the time that you are feeling relaxed and calm and that your breathing is deep and regular. Visualise yourself working quickly but calmly through the questions on the paper, aware all the time that your jaw and shoulder are relaxed and that you are free from excess tension.

3. Repeat the process every day or evening until the day of the exam. What you will be doing is persuading your subconscious mind to associate the image of the exam situation with the concept of relaxation and freedom from anxiety. And your subconscious mind is unable to distinguish between what is real and what is imagined. If you continue to feed in this imagined scene over a period of three weeks, the association will become permanent. If you ever had fears of your mind becoming blank when taking an exam, these fears will be eradicated by the superimposition of the new image – just as the old programme on an audio or video cassette is permanently erased when a new one is recorded over it.

Remembering names and faces

At first glance you might not think it terribly important that you are always able to put the right name to the right face. But ask any businessman or -woman and I am sure they will tell you otherwise. You are paying an individual a compliment when you are able to remember his name and this will automatically raise you higher in his estimation. As Dale Carnegie says in his 'Human Relations' course, 'The sweetest sound to any individual is the sound of his (her) own name.'

There are two stages to this process (and they both allow you to have a little fun):

- Remembering the name
- Linking the name to the appropriate person

Remembering names

Working on the premise that the more ridiculous something is, the easier it is to recall, here is an opportunity to let your imagination run riot by allowing the names to create images in your mind. Sometimes, of course, this is simple as certain names actually have meanings of their own – names like Martin, Daisy, Mark, Brown and Driver. Others will require a little more creative thought on your part, but there is no name for which you cannot find a visual image, even if it means dividing it up into sections or syllables, as is often necessary with foreign names.

In most cases you will have two names to work on – the forename and the surname. So, once you have created the two images you must find a link between them. Remember to render this as memorable as possible by making it amusing. Let's take a few examples, using names picked at random (with apologies to any reader upon whose name I might unwittingly have chanced). The images described will be those which came automatically into *my* mind, but remember that for this system to be really effective, you must use your own visual skills to create your own pictures.

Adrian Warburton: Hadrian in full armour, marching along his Wall ready to go to war. On his breastplate is the most enormous button sewn on with bright red thread.

Mary Sylvester: A bride (Mary = marry) in a white gown with a veil and bouquet. The fabric of her dress is so fine that you can see a silver vest shining through it.

Arthur Mansfield: Half a man (sliced vertically head to toe) hopping happily around a large green field.

Give yourself some practice by selecting any list of names – perhaps from the telephone directory, perhaps from the list of characters in a radio or television play – and see what pictures come into your mind when you think of those names.

Linking names and people

Now remembering all these names is not going to do you much good if you are never sure which name belongs with which person. So, while creating your own mental image you also have to link it with the owner of the name.

Really look at the person whose name you wish to remember. See Adrian in his suit of armour; picture Mary in her flowing white gown; and decide whether it is to be Arthur's left or right half which is to do the field-hopping.

There is an added bonus to using this system, particularly if you are someone who is often overawed by others. How can Henry seem intimidating when every time you look at him you picture him with a big, fat hen sitting on his shoulder? Can Sally really wither you with a glance when you imagine coconuts being thrown at her head?

Remembering lists and random items

Have you seen those stage performers who ask members of the audience to call out the names of unrelated objects and are then able to remember those items in any order? They are using one of the oldest memory systems in existence – the peg-word system. This involves associating the random objects to a fixed series of words. Let's see how the system works.

A skilled performer will often use up to a hundred peg-words, but for the sake of this exercise we will just work on ten. Taking the numbers one to ten, invent a rhyming noun for each number. Mine are:

- One – bun
- Two – shoe
- Three – tree
- Four – door
- Five – hive
- Six – sticks
- Seven – heaven
- Eight – gate
- Nine – line
- Ten – hen

Once you have selected your own nouns (and they do not have to be the same as mine), learn them well. These will never change; they will always symbolise for you the numbers one to ten.

Think of ten random objects: perhaps a horseshoe, a nectarine, the Eiffel tower, a Christmas tree, a walking stick, a computer, a blackbird, a dandelion, a hamburger and a pocket watch. Now find a way of linking these objects with your chosen peg-words. As before, make the image outrageous rather than sensible. In other words, don't simply have a bun lying on a horseshoe; imagine a horse with four currant buns on its hooves. Your other associations might be:

- A pair of shoes stuffed to overflowing with nectarines
- A tree hung with dozens of miniature Eiffel towers
- A door with a Christmas tree in place of a knocker
- Lopsided bees staggering into their hive with the aid of walking sticks
- A home-made computer built entirely of sticks
- A surprised blackbird floating up to heaven on a fluffy white cloud
- Opening a gate to find your way blocked by a fifty-foot dandelion
- A line of hamburgers pegged out to dry
- A hen laying pocket watches instead of eggs

Having created those images, if someone were to ask you: 'What is item number eight?', your mind would automatically make the link between your gate and the dandelion.

You might feel that this system will be of little use to you other than as a way to impress your friends, but, both in the world of learning and away from it, there are innumerable occasions when you might wish to remember several different items. Once you have memorised your own pegwords, this will never again prove difficult.

6

Hearing and Listening

Just as there is a distinction to be made between seeing and observing, there is all the difference in the world between hearing something and really listening to it. The ability to listen – as opposed to hear – involves concentration. If you want to find out how few people really concentrate on what is being said, try this test on your friends. Read this piece aloud:

> A city businessman was closing the office at the end of the working day when a man rushed in and, pointing a gun at him, demanded money. The office safe was opened. The contents of the safe were put into a bag and the man sped away. A member of the police force was immediately called.

Now make the following eight statements. In each case there is a choice of three answers – 'true', 'false' or 'not stated'.

1. A man rushed in as the manager was closing the office
2. The robber was a man
3. The man did not demand money
4. The man who opened the safe was the manager
5. Somebody opened the safe
6. After the robber put the contents of the safe into the bag, he ran away
7. As soon as the robber had gone, a policeman was summoned
8. The only people mentioned in the story are the manager, the robber and the policeman

The answers are:

1. Not stated. (The city businessman was closing the office – he may not have been the same person as the manager.)

2. True

3. False

4. Not stated. (We do not know who opened the safe.)

5. True

6. Not stated. (We do not know who put the contents of the safe into the bag.)

7. Not stated. (The member of the police force could have been a man or a woman.)

8. Not stated. (There could be four people if the business-man and the manager were two different people. Also we do not know that the member of the police force was a man.)

I would be extremely surprised if anyone managed to give the right answer in every case. In fact, in all the Learning to Learn training seminars I have conducted over a period of years, I have *never* found a single person who did so. Why is this?

We all tend to hear what we *think* we hear. We make assumptions based on prior knowledge, belief and experience – but these assumptions may be faulty. In the case of the exercise above, it is not that people do not hear the words or that they do not understand what is being said to them; but they hear it on a superficial level. Because the text is so short and simple, they do not feel they have to make a real effort of concentration.

Concentration in listening

You know how it is when you listen to a boring speaker; your mind tends to wander and all sorts of other thoughts come into your head. As a result you take in very little of what is being said, even though, on one level, you hear every word.

It is far more difficult to concentrate when hearing than it is when seeing. If you are looking at something, it is possible to focus your attention upon that word or image and nothing else. If you are listening you may begin by paying full attention but, because you are seeing things at the same time, there is a tendency for your thoughts to follow the images rather than the sounds, images being easier to concentrate upon.

Even if we are face to face with the person who is speaking, it is quite possible for the mind to wander (particularly if we are not really interested in what is being said). We can end up thinking about what to have for supper or how to deal with a family problem.

Of course, since we do not dwell in a cocoon of silence, there will always be other noises around us and this can make concentration extremely difficult, even if we find the subject matter interesting. In fact, the more we allow those distracting sounds to annoy us, the more aware of them we become and our ability to focus our attention on what we were listening to disappears. And yet, on the occasions when we manage to sustain that concentration, the extraneous noises somehow seem to disappear from our consciousness.

Once again, it is a case of concentration being far easier to maintain when we are interested in what we hear. A tired mother may sleep in front of the television or through a raging thunderstorm, and yet wake instantly should her new baby begin to whimper. Her child *matters* to her, and so her mind is ever alert to any sound it makes.

If you want to improve your listening concentration, as with seeing and observing you must find a way of making the subject matter important and of interest to you. Perhaps, because it is part of a wider subject you wish to study, you can develop an interest in what is being said, however dull the speaker may be. Indeed, it is better to sit there mentally taking an opposing view than drift off in a sea of vague thoughts. At least you will be more likely to listen to what is being said, if only so that you can find another bone of contention.

There are a few exercises you can practise to improve your listening concentration:

- As you walk along the street, set yourself the task of picking out one type of sound from the cacophony around you. You may choose to listen out for all the children's voices or all the music coming from shops or car radios. If you concentrate, you will soon find that you become aware only of the sounds you seek and manage to ignore every other noise, no matter how intrusive.

- Buy a record of birdsong (or borrow one from a record library). Learn to distinguish between the sounds made by the different species of bird – you won't manage it without a high degree of concentration, which will later stand you in good stead in other areas of life.
- When listening to a speaker, either in person or on the radio or television, realise that he or she will have spent time planning and structuring what he has to say. As you listen, analyse how he has done this and how his points progress, whether you agree with him or not.

Improving your listening concentration

Clear the decks before you begin. Put out of reach (preferably out of sight) anything with which you are likely to fiddle while listening. You do not need any distractions around you. Similarly you must clear your mental decks. If you have a problem on your mind or something you know you have to remember, make a deliberate effort to set it aside (write it down first, if that helps) so that your mind is free to concentrate upon what you are going to hear.

Remind yourself that everything we learn has a purpose, even if that purpose is not immediately obvious. It may be that the benefit to you of what you are about to hear will be blatantly evident. Or it may be that, once you have heard it, you will decide that the information has no relevance in your life – but if you don't listen to it, how will you ever know?

Try to link what you hear with other senses. If you are listening to a record of birdsong, it may help you to have the appropriate pictures in front of you. If a speaker or lecturer is talking about a particular subject, study any slides or illustrations that may be presented. By doing this you will prevent your mind from being distracted by other sights around you.

Because your brain is capable of functioning considerably more quickly than anyone is able to speak, you will have time mentally to 'file' what you hear, to observe any actions and illustrations and to realise how the new information increases your own store of knowledge. Or, indeed, you will have time to decide precisely why you disagree with what is being said. If you do not use your brain in this way, you will find that the 'spare' time will automatically be used to allow your mind to wander on to other thoughts.

Dull speakers and lecturers often do great disservice to interesting facts. It may help if you can concentrate on the content and import of what is being said and not spend too much time being judgmental about voice quality and delivery.

If your mind still tends to wander, you can always play a guessing game. Try to guess what the speaker is going to say next and wait to see if you are right – but don't become so intent on the game and your successes that you forget to listen to what follows.

Do what you can to ignore all distractions, both visible and audible. There will always be someone in the audience with an irritating cough. You may hear drilling from road works outside the building. The speaker may put on and remove his spectacles every few seconds – but try not to count! I once missed the whole content of a talk because I was so fascinated by the way the speaker seemed to 'dance' on stage – as he talked he would take two steps forward, two steps back, one to the side and so on. I was on the edge of my seat because, had he made a mistake in his routine, he might well have fallen off the stage altogether!

Remembering that images are far more likely to remain in the mind than words, see if you can use the spare time mentioned earlier to translate the words into mental pictures. Then you will have two senses to rely upon when it is time to recall the content of the talk or lecture.

Look at an animal when it is poised to listen. It stands absolutely motionless, with its ears pricked up. You may not be able to do much about your ears, but you can sit still with your back straight. If you lean slightly forwards and look at the speaker, you are more likely to concentrate on what he is saying.

You may decide that it would be helpful to take notes while listening, but try and restrict what you write to key words and points. In so doing you will have enough information to make sense when you come to read it through afterwards, but you will not be so busy attempting to scribble down every word that you don't take in the meaning of what is being said (see Chapter 8). Sometimes just deciding *what* you should write is sufficient to focus your mind upon the subject matter.

Don't fall into the trap of planning your own question or reply while someone else is speaking – whether in a learning or social situation. If you listen to what is being said and link it in your own mind with what you already know, you will be quite capable of putting any point you wish when the time comes. We have all been present when members of a class or an audience have asked the speaker a question which everyone else knows he has already covered in his talk.

If you have taken notes, go through them as soon after the class or lecture as possible. Make sure you understand what was being said, and add words here and there to make things clearer if this seems necessary. You might even decide to make a thought-flow chart at this point to fix matters in your own mind.

It always pays to ask questions at the time if you think there is anything about what you have been listening to that you do not fully understand – whether a lecture has been delivered or you have been given directions to a place which is new to you. I have found when working with students that many people are reluctant to say the words 'I don't understand' in case this makes them appear foolish before others. If this applies to you, there are a few openings you can use to your questions, such as:

- 'So does that mean that . . . ?'
- 'Am I right in thinking that . . . ?'
- 'Just to be sure I understand, are you saying . . . ?'

I'm sure you can think of others for yourself.

Remember, too, that if there was something you did not fully understand, it is quite likely that others did not understand it either. Donald Weiss of the American Management Association tells the story of an annual conference where all the speeches were long and dry. Some psychologists – to prove a point – had hired an actor to deliver a lecture. Although he would give this talk with expression and authority, the actor would in fact be talking rubbish. Intermingled with the ordinary words would be any number of natural-sounding but invented ones (after the fashion of the comedian Stanley Unwin). At the end of the conference, delegates, impressed presumably by the actor's animation and liveliness of delivery, said that this had been the best lecture of all.

Of course, had they been concentrating on the content of what was being said, had they been taking notes of key words, or had they been willing to query anything they did not understand, those delegates would not have been so easily fooled.

One way in which you can practise to ensure that such a thing does not happen to you is to ask a friend or colleague to spend three or four minutes giving you some information. At the end of that time, see if you can repeat the content of what was said back to the original speaker. Believe me, it is much harder than you would think. But it is interesting to see how, with practice, most people can become quite adept at grasping the content of what has been said.

7

Improving Your Reading

You may wonder how it is possible to improve your reading when it is something you have been doing for years. You may even be questioning the necessity of doing so – after all, you haven't encountered any real problems so far. But reading usually plays a great part in any course of study, so it must be beneficial to learn how to read in a way which is both speedier and more efficient.

The object of this chapter is to teach you how to increase the speed at which you read and also how to read to learn by extracting key words and facts from the text. This will facilitate both comprehension and revision. You will also find exercises to increase the efficiency of your sight and reduce the strain upon your eyes.

How your eyes work

If you are going to improve the way in which you use your eyes, it is necessary first of all to know a little about how they work. It is important to remember that, if you are looking at an object and that object is still, then your eyes also must be still. But if the object is moving, your eyes must move too. If you have ever tried to read the name of a station from the window of a moving train, you will know what I mean. The sign bearing the name is stationary and your eyes are moving, so all you see is a blur. (There is a way of doing it, however; if you concentrate upon the sign before you draw level there will be a brief instant when you are facing the name and your eyes will be still – not for long, but just enough time to be able to read what is written there.)

The difficulty that arises when reading is that your eyes have to work in two ways. They have to move in order to travel along the lines of words, and yet they also have to stop in order to read the individual words written or printed there. There are, however, several ways in which you can speed up your reading, bearing these eye movements in mind.

You also have greater peripheral vision than you might think. You may be looking straight ahead but you can also see much of what is to the right and left of you, even if you do not pay much attention to it at the time. You will see, as you read on, how it can be beneficial to increase the awareness of what is taken in by this peripheral vision.

Speed up your reading

Any student will realise that life can be made much easier if he or she can learn to read more quickly while still understanding what has been read. There is no point in being able to read rapidly if you come to the end of the section of text only to find that you have not absorbed any of its meaning.

If we take a piece of text which does not include complicated technical language or scientific formulae, the average reading speed for an adult is 100–300 words per minute. Yet, with practice, it is not difficult for the majority of people to increase this speed to 500–600 words per minute and dramatically cut the time spent on this part of studying.

If you are to increase the speed at which you read, you obviously need to know how quickly you are capable of reading at the present time. What follows is an extract from my book *Elements of Visualisation*, which you can use as a test piece because it is written in ordinary, non-technical language and is not interrupted by diagrams or illustrations. Use a stop-watch or some other accurate method of measuring the time, and see how long it takes you to read the text.

With each day that passes, it is becoming more generally accepted that our mental state has a great effect upon our physical health. Naturally that effect can be for better or for worse. It is an acknowledged fact, for instance, that someone who is unhappy or depressed is far more likely to suffer from a cold than someone who is feeling content with life.

Speaking of colds, you will always find some people who proudly proclaim 'I never get a cold' – and indeed they do not. And yet, unless they are living a peculiarly isolated existence, these people must come into contact with the same number of germs and viruses as everyone else. Why then are they not coughing and sneezing or suffering from other typical symptoms of a cold? You have already been given the answer to that question – they *know* that they are not going to have a cold and that knowledge is sufficient to reinforce their immune system and make the belief fact.

The same thing works in reverse. We have all met the individual who says 'I must be run down. If ever there is a cold or flu about, I am always the one to catch it.' And catch it they do. They spend a large part of the winter (and often the summer too) with a blocked nose, rheumy eyes and a throbbing head.

But what exactly does it mean when someone claims to be 'run down'? Simply that their immune system is not functioning effectively – and that is something which can be most effectively corrected by positive visualisation.

I am not attempting to convey here the impression that visualisation makes it possible to do away with doctors, surgeons and therapists at one fell swoop. Far from it. What it *can* do is work hand-in-hand with other forms of treatment, making them more efficient and allowing the patient to participate in his own recovery. Much of what you will find written in this chapter is effective only when you have consulted the relevant expert to find out precisely what is wrong with you. Of course, self-diagnosis exists, but it is often a dangerous exercise as the patient not only has insufficient knowledge of the workings of his body but, in addition, is frequently in a despondent state which makes it even harder for him to be objective about his symptoms.

The most successful form of treatment – whether by orthodox or complementary medicine – is one which cares for the patient holistically. That is to say, the patient as a whole is treated – as opposed to the symptom. There is no point in giving someone a pill which will disperse a pain in one part of his body if it is merely going to reappear in another.

Dealing with Pain: This is an area where one must be very,

very careful. It is quite a simple matter to use the power of your mind to dissolve pain – but it can be a dangerous thing to do.

The piece you have read is just over five hundred words long, so you should now be able to work out your average reading speed.

Time taken	Average reading speed
5 minutes	100 words per minute
4 minutes	125 words per minute
3 minutes	165 words per minute
2 minutes	250 words per minute
1 minute	500 words per minute

Now let's see what we can do to increase that speed:

1. *Eye movement:* If the eye movement of a poor reader is studied, there are various traits which can be compared with the eye movement of a good reader:
   - the eyes of a poor reader will only read one word each time they stop moving
   - passage along the line of text will be jerky rather than smooth
   - the poor reader will often go back to reread a word or phrase at which he has already looked.

   What you need to do, therefore, is train yourself to read several words each time your eyes stop moving and ensure that the general flow of your eye movement as it travels along the lines of print is smooth and that you do not look back at words you have already passed. This will naturally take practice – and indeed you may find that initially it feels unnatural to you and even that it seems to slow you down. But do persevere. Just like any other muscles, the muscles around the eyes can be trained to work in the way you wish.

2. *Using a pointer:* Do you remember when you first learned to read as a child? You probably put your finger on each word as you concentrated upon it and then

mouthed the word to yourself as you read it. Then you were taught that it is more 'grown up' to abandon both these habits. Well, the mouthing or speaking of the words is definitely not to be encouraged; it would certainly slow you up, as you can read far more quickly than you can speak. But the idea of a pointer is not necessarily a bad one – although using your finger is not a good idea as it is too large an object to be helpful. Nor do you need to point to each word as you go, which would only reinforce the bad habit of reading one word at a time. Try using the point of a pencil and pass it smoothly down the right-hand side of the passage of text; it will help to keep your attention focussed upon the correct line and ensure a much smoother eye movement than you might otherwise have.

If you have doubts about the efficacy of using a pointer, just think of all those people (perhaps in pre-calculator days) who would run a pen or pencil down the side of a column of figures they were adding. It was an aid to concentration and reduced the wandering of eyes. In just the same way it can help when reading and concentrating upon the printed word.

Using a pointer is not necessary if you are simply reading for fun or relaxation, when it doesn't really matter if you miss a few words as long as you grasp the gist of what is written. But when you are studying a piece of text and it is full of facts which you need to know, you want to be certain you do not skip anything. This is where the pointer comes in useful.

Now go back to the piece of text you read earlier. Use a pointer to aid the smooth progress of your eyes along the lines, and try to read several words at one time. Time yourself and you will probably find that you have already increased your reading speed. If you can do that in so short a time, just think what you will achieve when you have had more time to practise.

Reading is a habit

Anyone can learn to read more quickly. Don't think that, because you were labelled a 'fast' or 'slow' reader as a child, that label needs to have any effect on you as you grow up. Too many people adapt themselves to the self-image forced upon them by earlier, and often thoughtless, pigeon-holing. There is nothing at all to prevent you improving yourself and discarding that earlier classification completely.

Get into the habit of frequent reading. Read anything you can lay your hands on – newspapers, magazines, books – even if it is only for a short period each day. The more you read, the speedier your reading will become.

Reading to learn

Setting the scene

Where you choose to study a book can be important. Most of us like to read in bed – or even in the bath – and, while this may be suitable for casual reading, it is not really appropriate if a serious purpose is involved.

Ideally you should sit at a table. You need an upright posture, although you should aim to be relaxed rather than stiff or rigid. Sitting up straight enables you to breathe correctly from your diaphragm and therefore ensures that more oxygen is carried to the brain. This in turn helps you to remain alert and to think more clearly.

The lighting in the room should be efficient, but not so bright that it hurts your eyes. Fluorescent lights are not a good idea, as the lack of fluctuation in the light can be tiring and lead to eye strain if you intend to read for a prolonged period of time. Try not to sit in such a way that your body casts a shadow over the text upon which you are concentrating, even if this means changing the position of the furniture.

Never begin any serious period of study without making sure that you have a pen and notepad close at hand and also a reasonable dictionary. Apart from these items, it is best to keep your desk or table as free from clutter as possible as the psychological effect of a clear surface is an aid to a clear-thinking mind.

The optimum distance between the text and your eyes should be 16–24 inches (200–300 cm). If you cannot read clearly at this distance (with spectacles if you normally use them), it may be time to have your eyes checked or your prescription changed.

When you do begin a study session, ensure that you are sitting comfortably in your seat and then take a few deep breaths – breathing from your diaphragm rather than from the upper chest area. Check that your shoulders are relaxed, that your fists are not clenched or your jaws clasped rigidly together. If you can break the habit of sitting with your legs or ankles crossed, this will help too. It is impossible to be fully relaxed in such a position.

While you are reading, remember to stop and look up every now and then, giving your eyes the chance to focus on something far away. This will help to prevent tired or watery eyes at the end of a session.

Before you begin

If you are reading for study, then there are certain steps you should take before you even begin to look at the words on the page:

- Remind yourself why you are reading at all. All reading, in the context of learning, is for a purpose. It is to enhance your knowledge, to enable you to develop your own thoughts and opinions by blending fresh ideas and facts with existing knowledge.
- Spend ten minutes looking at the book in general. Study the chapter headings and the sub-headings. Look at the list of contents and the index. Flick through the pages, noting the illustrations and the diagrams. Ten minutes spent in this way will give you a fair idea of what that particular book is about – and it might even prevent you wasting a great deal of valuable time if, in fact, you

decide that the book in question is not going to be of any great use to you.

- Once you have found a book which is suitable for your needs, divide it into practical modules by deciding what portion of it you will study at any one sitting. This will naturally depend upon the subject you are studying and the type of book you have before you. You will obviously be able to cope with far larger chunks of a history or English book than you will if it is full of scientific or mathematical data. With some books, it is sufficient to read them in enough depth to glean information; with others you will have to be able to repeat formulae or paraphrase passages.

  Try and estimate how much you will be able to cover in the amount of time you have set yourself. This may be a matter of trial and error at first, but you will soon come to know how much you can cope with in one session. The significant thing to take into account, of course, is not how many pages of text you were able to cover, but how much you can read while still being able to recall at will all the salient points covered. If you are over-optimistic in the beginning, just reduce your quota a little. It is far better to do this than to study inefficiently. After all, the whole object of the exercise is to learn from what you are reading.

- As I said above, learning involves the intermingling of newly acquired knowledge with information of which you are already aware. Before you start to study a new book or a new chapter, spend a few moments thinking about what you know of the topic in question. By bringing previous knowledge to the forefront of your mind, you will more easily be able to blend the old and new information.

What to do when reading

It is said that only 20 per cent of any book consists of new ideas or concepts. The remaining 80 per cent is there to give us a basic framework on which to build. In other words, every 'and', 'the' and 'therefore' is there to fill in the gaps between the pieces of information. So, although your eyes will naturally pass over all these words – and indeed they will help you to make sense of what you read – none the less the number of words or phrases that you actually have to remember in any one section of the book is comparatively small.

If you understand the meaning of what you read you will be able to explain it in your own words. You are not trying to reproduce, word for word, what the author has said – in fact it is highly unlikely that the author himself would be able to do that.

Be interested

You will find it extremely difficult to retain what you read unless you are interested in it. This can present a problem when you have set books to study which may not be of your choice. If you cannot arouse any interest in a particular book, tell yourself that other people have found it interesting and try and work out what they could have seen in it. Ask yourself the point of the passage you are studying. If you find this difficult to answer, stop and think about it. Try looking again at the introduction to the book or to that particular section.

Key words

As you read, get into the habit of continuously looking out for the key words or facts in the text. These may be single words, new pieces of information, dates and so on. The average page of text can be reduced to approximately ten to fifteen key words. When you come to the end of your selected piece, make a list of these key words and then create from them your own thought-flow chart so that the concept makes sense. This will prevent you lapsing into the tedious practice of 'learning by heart', as you will have thought things through sufficiently to be able to understand them and will therefore be able to retain the new information and recall it at will.

Try this exercise. While reading the following passage (taken from one of my articles on hypnosis) make a list of key words and phrases.

'But I heard every word . . .' How often this comment is made by someone who has just experienced hypnosis for the first time. It seems that almost everybody expects to be 'asleep' or 'unconscious' when hypnotised, whereas of course this is far from the truth.

Perhaps the best way of describing what it feels like to be hypnotised is to call it a cross between a deep relaxation and a light meditation – and the most important thing for any prospective patient to realise is that, at all times, he or she will be in complete control of the situation. Indeed, if he is determined not to be hypnotised, then nothing at all will happen. He will be able to hear every word spoken, to understand all that is said and, if at any time he is not happy with what the therapist is saying, all he has to do is open his eyes and the session is over.

But how can any benefit be derived from being relaxed and listening to someone talking to you? The point is, of course, that when your body and your conscious mind are in a state of relaxation it is possible for the words of the therapist to reach your subconscious mind. And it is your subconscious which, feeding upon all the experiences which have ever touched you and the influences exerted upon you by all the people and events in your life, affects your present actions and reactions.

What have you put on your list? Mine would read as follows:

Hypnotherapy
- expects
- asleep/unconscious
- relaxation/meditation
- control
- hear/understand
- benefit
- subconscious
- experiences (people and events)

Now take the list and create from it a thought-flow chart on the topic of hypnotherapy. It will probably look some-

thing like the one which follows (although there is no harm
in adding some ideas of your own if they help your understanding of the topic).

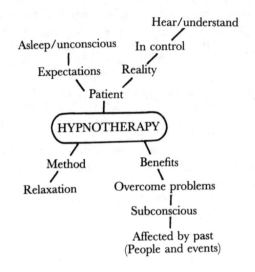

Sticking points

There may be times when you suddenly realise that,
although you have been reading the words, you have not
actually taken in the meaning of the text. There are several
possible explanations for this:

1. You are tired. If this is so, you would be better advised
   to bring that session to a close and try again later or
   even the following day. Not only will you make yourself
   even more tired by persevering, but you will be unlikely
   to glean anything from the words you read. This in turn
   may cause you to become disenchanted with the subject
   or annoyed with yourself – both of which negative emotions are a total waste of energy.
2. You have set yourself too great a task. Perhaps you have
   divided the book into sections which are too large for
   you to cope with. Struggling on would be useless. Better
   by far to reduce the amount of work to be tackled at
   any one time.

3. The text is difficult. You have several options here:

- go back over the part you have just read and see whether the meaning becomes clearer
- write down what you think are the main points covered, so that you can see whether you have understood them
- try another book; there are some very boring authors, you know!
- press on for a while and see if the next passage helps to clarify the earlier one
- ask for help from a tutor or an expert in the subject you are studying

The most important thing is not just to sit there becoming disillusioned and despondent. There is always something to be done to ease the situation.

Vocabulary

How much you are hampered by a restricted knowledge of vocabulary depends greatly upon the type of reading you are doing and the topic you are studying.

If the text is of a general (as opposed to a technical) nature, it probably will not matter if you come across the occasional word with which you are not familiar. Provided it does not ruin your understanding of the passage you are reading, then you can just pass over it without stopping. If you find the word occurring more than once, however, jot it down in your notebook and look it up afterwards.

If the book or paper you are studying contains several words of a specialist or technical nature, you will obviously be aware of this in advance. Before you even begin to read, take some time to skim through the text, picking out any technical language or unfamiliar terms. Write these down and look up the meanings. You can then keep the list beside you as you read so that your progress is not halted.

If your vocabulary is not large enough, your reading speed is likely to be considerably reduced. You can help yourself to overcome this stumbling block by improving your general vocabulary. Allocate a regular time to this. Keep a vocabulary notebook in which you can list any words you come across which are unfamiliar to you, using a dictionary to discover their meanings. If you keep this note-book in your bag or pocket, you can look at it in all those otherwise idle moments – when you are waiting for a train, for example.

After a reading session

When you come to the end of the section you have chosen to study, sit back and ask yourself what the author was try-ing to say. Do you agree with it? Would you be able to explain the ideas to someone else, using your own words?

When you are working out the length of your study peri-ods, remember to allow time for making notes after you have finished reading. If you can get into the habit of *always* writing something – even if only in note form – after a ses-sion of studying, you will help to fix what you have read in your mind and therefore make remembering it less of an effort.

The method in which you take these notes is up to you (see Chapter 8 for suggestions). In some way you have to paraphrase what you have just read. You may wish to jot down the ideas and concepts as words or phrases to ensure that you understand them. If there is any point about which you are doubtful, this is the time to review it by going back and looking at the text again. If you leave uncertainties to mount up, you will eventually reach the stage where you lose sight of the meaning of the book altogether.

Once you are sure that you have grasped the meaning of what has been written, create a thought-flow chart to illus-trate it. This serves two purposes. For one thing it will help you to understand not simply what the ideas are but how they came about and their natural progression. For another, it is far easier, when it comes to revising, to study a selec-tion of thought-flow charts containing the essentials of what you need to know than to reread book after book.

Studying a foreign language

With the increased links between Britain and the rest of the European Community, many people are now setting out to learn a foreign language. Some will be businesspeople anxious to enter wholeheartedly into the single European market; others may wish to take advantage of the Channel Tunnel and buy a home abroad.

Whatever your reason, it has been found that, when reading words in an unfamiliar language, it is beneficial to have a translation printed alongside. Even though you may not choose to refer to the translation itself, while your concentrated vision is taking in the words written in one language, your peripheral vision will automatically be aware of the translation and so you will be learning subconsciously. (I am assuming here that your aim is to be able to converse in that language – whether in the boardroom or the local shops – and not to study its great literature.)

In addition, this is one area of learning where the sections should be kept relatively small – probably no more than about five sentences at a time.

Eye exercises

You can do simple exercises to help keep the muscles around the eyes working efficiently. This will assist in preventing tiredness and eye strain as well as actual impairment of vision.

1. When you are reading, pause every now and then and look at something in the distance – perhaps the view from the window. Intense concentration upon the printed page can cause headaches as well as tension around the eyes.
2. Make sure that you blink your eyes when reading. When we concentrate on something all our muscles grow far more tense, and when we are tense we do not blink. Indeed, one of the ways in which you can tell whether

someone is nervous, even if they are putting on a wonderful act of bravado, is by watching their eyes. That unblinking stare is a great give-away. So, every now and then, look up from the book and blink several times; your eyes will be lubricated and less likely to grow tired.

3. Relax. The more relaxed you are, the less tension will be present in your body as a whole – and therefore the less tension there will be around your eyes. In many instances defective vision and eye strain are caused not by any malfunction of the eyes themselves but by excess tension in the muscles around them. Practitioners of the Bates method of eye improvement, who teach a special system of exercises for these muscles, have found that the patient is often able to use spectacles of a lesser strength or even, in some cases, to give up using them altogether.

You can practise any basic method of relaxation, either alone or as part of a group. There are even cassettes to help you (details on p. 158). Don't just wait until you are about to sit down to study; try and make relaxation a part of your daily routine, even if you are only able to spend ten or fifteen minutes on it. I can promise that you will find it well worth while – and not only from the point of view of your eyes. When you are relaxed and breathing properly more oxygen is able to flow to the brain, enabling it to work more efficiently. So your studying will be helped in many ways.

4. To assist flexibility of those muscles around your eyes, try this exercise from time to time. Hold a pencil, point uppermost, at arm's length. Make sure the point is at eye level and focus your attention upon it. Slowly and smoothly bring the pencil towards you until it is about eight inches from your nose (before you go cross-eyed) and then, equally smoothly, return it to its original position. Do this three times.

5. If you feel that your eyes are tired, cup your hands and place them over the eye area (without touching the eyes themselves). Leave them in that position for about thirty seconds while you breathe deeply and evenly. Repeat this five times.

6. Exercise your eyes as you would your body. Look straight ahead (but not towards a bright light). Now, without moving your head, look up as high as you can and then down as low as possible. Look as far to the right as you can and then to the left before returning to your original position. Wait for a moment or two and then repeat the exercise, doing it three times in all.

7. There is much to be said for the old remedy of placing cool pads over your closed eyes to relieve any build-up of tension. This is particularly effective if you have been driving in bright light for any length of time. You can use pads soaked in water or in a special eye lotion – or you can use slices of cucumber.

8. Remember that we do not just see what is straight ahead but we also have peripheral vision and can take in a good deal of what is to the left and right. Try this exercise when sitting in the front seat of a car (but not when you are the driver!). Look straight ahead at the road in front of you, but notice as much as possible of what is to the left and right. See how much you are able to take in. This will stand you in good stead when you are trying to increase your reading speed as, with practice, it becomes possible to look straight down the middle of the page and see enough of what is to the right and left to make perfect sense of the text.

8
Writing and Note-taking

Perhaps we should start by asking why you need to take notes at all. Presumably you want to be able to remember what has been said, and you may need to revise for an examination. It is far better, for these purposes, to take your own notes rather than have them dictated to you while you copy them down unthinkingly. If you take the notes yourself, you will have to think about what you are writing and understand what is being said. You will also put them in such a way that you are able to make sense of them afterwards.

In this chapter we are going to look at various aspects of writing as a part of the learning process. Points to be covered include:

- how to increase your writing speed while maintaining (and improving) legibility
- taking notes – whether while attending lectures or while reading for research
- reproducing – to include setting out ideas for revision, essays and reports
- handwriting, grammar and so on – still important, as weakness in this area can cause you to lose vital marks in examinations and credibility if writing a formal report
- writing essays, reports and theses

How to speed up your writing

For most of us, learning time is at a premium. The student may have many different subjects to study; the busy mother or returner to work will have to fit studying into a day where every moment is already spoken for; for the business-man or -woman it is something which often comes at the end of an extremely hectic day. Anything we can do to speed things up, provided it is not done at the expense of acquiring relevant knowledge, must be helpful.

What to use

If you regularly take notes at lectures or seminars, make sure that you have a reasonable pad to work on rather than a tiny notebook or loose scraps of paper. Many people like a shorthand notebook, as you can get a reasonable amount on each sheet and the wire spiral keeps all the pages together. Others prefer a large A4 pad or one with punched holes to fit a ring-binder. The disadvantage of these pads is that, as you turn each page, it is likely to become detached from the rest of the pad. In any case, most people need to rewrite their notes after a lecture; that is the time to transfer it on to paper with punched holes so that separate sheets can be inserted in the right place in your ring-binder.

When using a shorthand notebook, try and develop the technique practised by professional shorthand writers. They gently slide up the page they are writing on so that they do not lose momentum as they flick it over when they reach the bottom line.

If you intend to write quickly, it is best not to use a pen-cil. One of the tricks of rapid note-taking is to use only very light pressure on the paper – there would be a danger of pencil strokes becoming so faint that they would be difficult to read. Better by far to use a pen – but do make sure it is comfortable to hold. There are many gimmicky pens avail-able which may be fun to own but which can slow down your note-taking considerably. It doesn't matter whether you choose a fountain pen or a ballpoint. A good ballpoint often flows more easily when you are writing at speed, but do keep a spare one handy in case it dries up.

Increasing your speed

The average writing speed for an adult is between twenty-five and thirty-five words (of five letters each) per minute. Repeated practice, writing for one or two minutes at a time to begin with, should enable you to increase your speed considerably. There are several things you can do to help you achieve this:

1. Before you even begin, make sure that you are sitting comfortably. You should be in an upright position while remaining as free from tension as possible.
2. Hold your pen fairly loosely. This will enable you to write more quickly and will prevent your hand becoming stiff or painful.
3. Use abbreviations. There are several ways of doing this, but it goes without saying that you must be able to make sense of them afterwards:

- Miss out vowels. It is surprisingly easy to get into the habit of doing this when note-taking, and you should have no difficulty in reading the notes back afterwards. Try this: Whn dggng in th grdn, t s bettr t hv a frk f th rght sze.
- Leave out unnecessary words such as 'the', 'and' and 'but'.
- Abbreviate the most obvious words:
    info – information
    (im)poss – (im)possible
    selec – selection
    govt – government
    co – company

Do be careful of any clashes, such as 'diff' which could be an abbreviation for either 'difference' or 'difficulty'. The same care is needed when using initial letters; you are unlikely to become confused when using PM for both *P*rime *M*inister and *P*reventative *M*edicine because they are not likely to appear in the same context. But what about PC for both *P*olice *C*ommissioner and *P*olice *C*onstable?

There are certain accepted signs which can be used as abbreviations for words. For example:

+ in addition to
− without
∴ therefore
∵ because

You will also be able to get into the habit of abbreviating those words which relate specifically to the subject you are studying. In the case of natural medicine, for example, you might find:

acu − acupuncture
hyp − hypnotherapy
ref − reflexology
hom − homoeopathy
thy − therapy
thst − therapist

At a lecture

Always start your notes by writing the date, the title or subject of the lecture and the name of the lecturer. This may seem an obvious statement, but it is amazing how we all think we are going to remember things and then find later that these details have escaped us. Keep any handouts and file these with your notes.

To take reasonable notes, you really need to listen to what is being said and to understand its sense and meaning. This takes concentration, as you have to follow the lecturer's train of thought and progression of ideas. Try and understand what he or she is saying, even if you do not always agree with it.

If you miss something, leave a large gap in your notes or put a large cross. Don't allow yourself to panic, or you will never be able to establish a reasonable rhythm again. As soon as the session is over, ask the lecturer about the missed point if that is possible. If it is not, ask another student (preferably one whose level of understanding you trust).

Rewrite your notes as soon as possible after the lecture

while everything is still fresh in your mind. You really will not remember it clearly the following week, however much you think you will. (A rewriting technique is described below.)

The repetitive process involved in (a) listening, (b) taking notes and (c) rewriting will in itself be an aid to learning and retention.

Rewriting

We have already seen how learning involves the blending of new information with what you already know. If you use a ring-binder and paper with punched holes you will be able to assist this blending process by inserting each set of notes with the most appropriate of your former ones.

Because you do not know, at the time of rewriting, whether you will at some later date discover titles of books or papers which can enhance and increase your knowledge, it is a good idea to leave a wide margin on each side of your writing and also plenty of space between lines. These later pieces of information can then be added without the inconvenience of further rewriting or of confusing cross-referencing.

Create thought-flow charts

As you go along, try and create a thought-flow chart to accompany each new piece of rewriting. Not only will it help to fix any relevant facts in your mind, but you will be able to reassure yourself that you have really understood all that you have heard or read. By the time you come to revise, you may find that these thought-flow charts are all you need. If you are undertaking a long course of study, however, you will probably also need the backup of your rewritten notes.

Thought-flow charts are particularly valuable for the businessman or -woman who may not have the time to go through pages of written notes whenever they wish to look up what they have learned. Suppose, for example, you wish to write and report and need to be sure that you have covered all the relevant points. Your list of key words might be as follows:

Content
Structure
Language
Presentation

and the chart itself would look something like this:

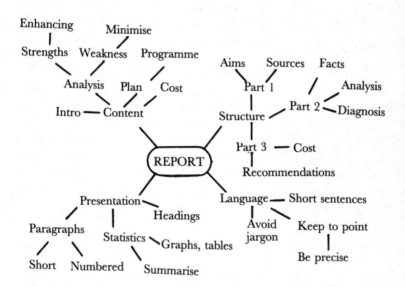

Keep details of sources

During a lecture or presentation you may be given titles of relevant books, papers and so on which will be helpful to you – or you may discover them in the course of your own research. When making notes from such sources, be sure to keep a record of titles and authors. You will also find it useful to take a note of where you found the source, of its

ISBN or library number and certainly of important chapter and page numbers.

Let the facts stand out

When making notes for your own revision, don't write great, long sentences and paragraphs – you might just as well set yourself a book to read. You will have to find a format which appeals to you and then stick to it – and the only way of doing this is to try various layouts and see which is most suitable for your purposes. But you need to divide what you have learned into headings, sub-headings, sections and sub-sections. Here is one way of doing it, but do vary it if you prefer another method:

SUBJECT   (capitals and underlined, possibly highlighted)
Subheading   (underlined)

1. First section (numbered and underlined)
   a) First fact
   b) Second fact
   c) Third fact

2. Second section
   a) First fact
   b) Second fact

                  . . . and so on.

Follow the established structure

It is likely that a great deal of thought and planning will have gone into the lecture you have heard or the book you have been reading. The way in which the facts were assembled will have been quite deliberate and should present a natural train of thought. Unless you found the original subject confusing in its presentation, you will find it helpful to follow that same train of thought when rewriting your notes for revision.

Think about this structure before you even begin to set pen to paper. Be certain that you understand not only the facts themselves but their cause and effect. Ask yourself:

- What happened?
- What led up to it?
- What was the result – both short-term and long-term?
- What is the significance of these facts within the subject as a whole?

Update regularly

As further lectures or research help you to acquire additional information, be sure to put your notes on it in the appropriate place so that it enhances your existing knowledge on the subject. Now is the time to enlarge the thought-flow charts you have already drawn up, so that they incorporate any new sequences of thought.

Should you find that any part of your notes now becomes cluttered and confusing, it is well worth taking the time to clarify the points in your own mind and to rewrite where necessary. Constant review is all part of the learning process, and this further rewriting forces you to review that part of the subject.

The value of rewriting

- It proves that you have understood what you have read or heard and that you are able to express it in your own words.
- You will discover at a very early stage if there is confusion in your mind about any part of the topic.
- The physical act of writing things down – particularly in the form of headings, sub-headings and the like – helps to fix the main points in your memory.
- Your notes will form the basis for revision and for any essays or papers you need to write.

Writing essays

Although what follows is designed to help those who have to write essays, the majority of points apply equally to reports, theses and other forms of formal writing.

Why write an essay?

Sometimes, of course, you have no choice in the matter; the essay may be part of a term's work or the answer to a question in an examination. But there are benefits to you too:

- The physical act of writing, as you already know, helps you to retain the information you have studied. Just think how, once you have written a shopping list or details of an unfamiliar route, it seems to stay in your mind and you hardly have to refer to your piece of paper at all.
- Because an essay involves the gathering and assembling of facts, when you come to write it using your own words you will prove to yourself (as well as to others) that you have really understood what you have been studying.
- Searching for additional information when preparing to write an essay is in itself an important part of the learning process. It compels you to think about the topic and to use your sense of reasoning as you get ready to put forward your views. Whatever the subject, your understanding of it will be deepened and you will learn even more about it.

Before you begin

Putting pen to paper is only one part of essay writing. There are several things to think about before you reach that point.

Restrictions

With the exception of personal letters, most forms of writing are bound by some restrictions. Writers of books and articles know before they begin the approximate length of text required by their publisher. If you are writing an essay as part of an examination, you will have to calculate how long you have in which to do it and how best to use the time available. Even if it is part of term or course work, it will not be the only thing you have to do and – while I am not suggesting it should be skimped – you do have to leave time for other studies too. Similarly, if you are writing a paper to be presented at a conference, you are not going to be allowed an unlimited amount of time in which to put your points across. So, since it is far more difficult than you would think to cut a piece of written work drastically, bear such restrictions in mind before you begin.

The title

A title is always carefully chosen to allow you to make specific points and show that you understand what you have been learning. It is very unlikely that you will ever be asked to write all you know about any individual topic. If, when writing an essay, you address a different aspect of the subject, then however accurate your facts and however brilliant your writing, you will not have fulfilled the task set and you will lose vital marks. Similarly, if you have been asked to prepare a business proposal and you do not cover precisely the ground required, you are not going to satisfy a potential client. Spend some time contemplating the title. What exactly is it saying? Look at the individual words and underline any which are relevant. If a question is posed, your essay must answer it.

For the full-time student and for those studying for professional qualifications at all levels, there are certain words which are regularly used in essay titles, both in examinations and in work being set as part of a continuous assessment process. Each of these words has a specific meaning (see p. 112).

It is also important to note whether you have been asked to write 'briefly', 'concisely', 'in detail' or starting from a particular position. If you have, there is no point in doing anything other than what has been asked of you.

Collecting information

Not only is this an essential part of the preparation for any formal piece of writing, it is also helpful as part of your own revision of the subject. Go through all your own notes, including your thought-flow charts, as this will indicate the

Word given	What is required
Describe	A verbal description, incorporating diagrams or illustrations if appropriate
Discuss	Give views on a topic, including points both for and against. You will not necessarily be expected to take sides.
Compare	Show the similarities between the subjects
Contrast	Show the differences between the subjects
Outline	Give details only of the main points
Explain	Give a detailed explanation of how something works
Criticise	Assess and judge. Always give your reasons. (In a criticism you may take a positive or a negative view.)

link between different ideas. Spend some time researching additional material, remembering to write down titles of relevant books, papers and so on, and where you found them. As thoughts come to you, jot them down in any order – you can always put them in logical sequence afterwards. (It is quite a good idea to write these ideas on separate cards or pieces of paper. Then, when you come to prepare the writing in detail, you can move them around until you find a sequence which pleases you.)

Once you have acquired sufficient information, you need to make a detailed plan. Trying to work at a desk covered with open books and scraps of paper does *not* make for clear thinking!

Making a plan

Any well-constructed piece of writing consists of the introduction, the main body and the conclusion. Remember this when making your plan. You might like to begin by drawing up a thought-flow chart to ensure that you cover all relevant points and to remind yourself of the link between them. When it comes to making a written plan, use headings, sub-headings and numbered paragraph headings to help clarify your sequence of thought. (Keep these notes and thought-flow charts, even after you have finished; they will form a useful part of your revision notes or a basis for future work.)

Decide upon the point you are making (referring back to the title) and ensure that your notes will enable you to do this. If you are to keep a constant thread running through your writing, you will have to link each paragraph to what has gone before. This helps to demonstrate to the reader your logical train of thought.

The introduction

An introduction need only consist of a single paragraph, the object being to show that you have fully understood the title given and to indicate the approach you intend to take and the conclusion you hope to make. This helps the reader to understand the direction in which he is being led.

The main body

Having decided upon the most logical sequence for the points you wish to make, keep to it as much as possible. It is all too easy to allow your thoughts to carry you off at a tangent (which is the main reason for assembling your ideas before you begin).

Be objective in your writing, putting your ideas as clearly as possible in what seems to you to be the most logical sequence. Be selective in your choice of words to ensure that you make your meaning clear to the reader. Remember to keep your sentences relatively short.

Where possible, use evidence gleaned from your research to back up your arguments. Phrases such as 'it has been shown . . .' are far too vague. The reader will want to know by whom, where and when. Research is an excellent way of stretching the boundaries of your knowledge of a subject – but don't copy great chunks, word for word, from other people's work. Not only is this plagiarism, it doesn't prove that you know anything at all.

A thesis or an essay is in part a test to see that you have understood the subject you have been studying, so remember to make use of what you have learned during the course itself. This will also be helpful for you, as it will indicate any gaps in your own knowledge as well as being valuable when you come to revise.

To ensure that you are not wasting your time and effort but are answering the question or covering the point raised in the title, keep glancing back at it and questioning the relevance of what you have written.

The same thing applies if you are writing a report or preparing a proposal. There is no point spending valuable time preparing a detailed piece of work only to have it sent back to you as 'inappropriate' or, even worse, to find that a prospective client has passed you over in favour of someone else.

Language

Suit the language you use to the type of work you are doing. Naturally there will be occasions when the subject calls for technical language, but it is normally advisable to keep your language as simple as possible. Remember, however, that there are words and phrases which are perfectly acceptable in speech which are not really suitable for writing in essays.

Grammar, punctuation and spelling

It has become fashionable in some areas to consider grammar, punctuation and spelling unimportant and not to deduct marks when they are poor. But, apart from the fact that many educationalists are now beginning to change their views, why should you want to let yourself down because of something which it is quite possible to learn? In addition, if your grammar and spelling are really bad, you run the risk that the reader will not understand what you are trying to say – so you may lose vital marks or fail to put your point across. You can obtain simple, straightforward books to help you with basic English grammar and, in any event, your writing does not have to involve complicated sentence construction; in fact, it will be far easier to understand if it does not. As for spelling, you can always keep a dictionary close at hand in order to check on any words about which you are unsure.

Readability

The best essays are immensely readable, as are the best reports. Readability does not simply involve a pleasing lay-out and legible handwriting or a typescript which does not contain too many errors – although these things do make life easier. The language you use and the style of your writing are important too. If you want the reader to understand the points you are trying to make, don't use long and little-used words or convoluted sentences. They would also make your own revision far more onerous at a time when you want things to be as straightforward as possible.

Giving an example to indicate your point is often far more valuable than paragraphs of theoretical discussion. These examples can be true or fictitious; you can always prefix the latter with 'Suppose . . . .'

At all costs avoid 'politician-speak', and do away with all unnecessary words. Consider the following and what they really mean:

'very true' – true
'equal halves' – halves
'three in number' – three
'at this moment in time' – now
'it could well be that' – perhaps

Using signposts

When you were preparing your notes, you put your points in what was to you a logical order. But remember that what appears logical to one person, with his experience, knowl-edge or belief, may not seem as logical to another. So make the link between your points obvious, or the reader may not follow your thought progression. Arguments have to flow naturally, so try to use verbal signposts to lead from one to another. A signpost is a way of reminding the reader of the point you have reached and of indicating the way you intend to proceed. It could be something as simple as: 'Having looked at ABC, we must now consider XYZ. . . .'

The conclusion

The conclusion should hark back to the title and indicate how what you have written has made the point or answered the question. For example, if you have been asked to 'discuss' without reaching a specific result from that discussion, then your conclusion should show how you have put both viewpoints.

The first draft

This may not be feasible under examination conditions, but at all other times – when writing an essay, an article, a thesis or any other piece of structured text – it is advisable to write an initial draft. This may seem like a lot of extra work for little reason, but I can assure you that this is not so. There are various benefits:

- When writing the first draft, you can allow the words to flow naturally so that you 'write from the heart' without having to worry about whether you have used the same word in three consecutive sentences or made the same point in four different ways.
- If this piece of writing is part of an ongoing course of study, each time you write it you will fix the information more firmly in your mind and therefore increase your knowledge.
- By reading your first draft to yourself (aloud if possible), you will easily spot the badly constructed sentence or the ambiguous phrase. This is particularly important if you are writing a paper to be given at a conference. As you read through your work, ask yourself the following questions:

1. Does it make sense? (This applies to each individual sentence and to the piece as a whole.)
2. Have I done what I set out to do (answer, discuss, evaluate or whatever)?
3. Does a logical sequence of thought flow through my writing – and is it obvious?
4. Have I included backup information (gleaned from research) and have I indicated the source of this information?
5. Is everything I have written relevant to what I have been asked?
6. (If part of a course) Have I shown that I have understood what I have been studying?
7. Is my style clear enough for the reader to follow my points without becoming confused?

Final copy

This is a corrected version of your first draft. Now is the time to tighten up sentences and eliminate anything which is irrelevant. Because you are simply making a good copy of what you have already written, you now have the opportunity to pay attention to legibility and layout so that your work is shown in its best light.

The point of essay writing as part of continuous assessment

1. To prove to the teacher/lecturer that you have understood what has gone before.
2. To show that you have the ability to collect and collate information from different sources.
3. To indicate that you are capable of analysing a situation – whether from a single viewpoint or from both sides of a question.

The point of a business proposal

1. To prove your understanding of the client's needs.
2. To show that it is possible to satisfy these needs and that you are the person to do it.
3. To explain how you will set about it.
4. To put forward your terms (fees and so on).

The point of a business report

1. To show your understanding of the present situation.
2. To demonstrate its strengths and weaknesses.
3. To offer proposals to enhance the former and eliminate the latter.
4. To present a plan and programme, including costs and benefits.
5. To summarise conclusions and recommendations.

9
Working with Numbers

Why bother yourself with numbers at all in everyday life? you might be thinking. After all, taking a calculator to the supermarket or office is such a commonplace that we don't even stop to think about it. It is true that in most cases it is possible to use a calculator, but the best way of developing and using your mind is by achieving a balance between the left and right sides of your brain. The simple exercises and theories described in this chapter will help you to do just that.

I wonder whether you are among the many people who insist that they are 'no good' with numbers or who feel that mathematics and calculation are beyond them. And yet we all have to deal with numbers every day and we do so without even realising what is happening.

So many of those who proclaim that they are unable to understand figures or to work with them in fact do so all the time. Consider the following examples:

- *The cook:* Whether dealing with imperial or metric measurements, anyone who cooks frequently can look at a recipe and know roughly the quantity of an ingredient represented by the figures written there. You will appreciate that 4 oz (or 100 g) of flour is not very much, while 2 pints (or 1½ litres) of milk is quite a lot. And this is before you even think of starting to weigh or measure.
- *The dieter:* You only have to hear that someone of 5ft 2ins weighs 12 stone and you know they are overweight. Similarly, someone of 6ft who weighs 8½ stone is certainly in need of fattening up.
- *The tennis fan:* Even if the only time you ever watch tennis is during Wimbledon fortnight each year, you will under-

stand what is meant if you are told that A beat B, 6−4, 6−3, 4−6, 4−6, 6−1.

- *The gardener:* You will immediately know that, if you are told the temperature tonight is going to fall to 30°F, it is time to light the heater in the greenhouse and protect your most vulnerable plants.
- *The listener to the weather forecast:* You might not know that 30°C is almost the same as 90°F, but you will know that it is pretty hot and it is time to reach for the sun barrier cream.

So you see you are actually dealing with figures all the time. It is just that you have become so used to doing so that you have ceased to think about it at all.

Even if you now accept that figures play quite a large part in your life, you might assume that you are not at ease with statistics. And yet you have probably already learned to understand graphs and diagrams, as these are often used to illustrate a point on television or in the newspaper. Take the very simple example below, which illustrates the monthly rainfall throughout the year in a particular region. You do not have to spend much time analysing the graph; a simple glance will tell you that there was quite a lot of rain in October and very little in July and August.

Perhaps you are still not convinced. You might think all these examples are fine but they have nothing to do with calculation, do they? Consider the following:

You are told you are going to get a pay rise of 10 per cent. Do you really mean to say you could not work out

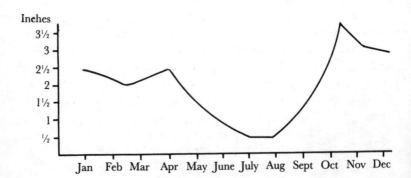

how much this is? And even if the percentage is less readily understandable, such as 6½ per cent, because it is a little over half of 10 per cent you would still know whether it was a great deal or a pittance.

Every time you eat soup from a spoon you are making several calculations. Your brain is working out the distance the spoon has to travel from the dish to your mouth, the amount of liquid the spoon will hold, and even the amount of energy needed to raise and lower your arm at the appropriate moments.

On the cricket pitch the fielder rushes to catch the ball. He does not have time to think about it but his brain is calculating the distance he has to run, the height of the ball from the ground, and the position in which he has to place his hands if he is not to miss the ball completely.

Even something as simple as stepping off a bus takes calculation if you are not to fall flat on your face. Your brain is automatically taking into consideration the distance between the step and the ground and the energy you need to exert in order to move your legs sufficiently to enable you to land safely.

When it comes to numbers, practice certainly does help to make perfect. An accountant once told me that he is able to read a set of accounts like a biography; he only has to turn the pages of a client's books and glance at the figures to know all about him and whether his business is doing well or not. And anyone who has to travel frequently on the railway is quite capable of 'reading' a train timetable to find out which platform to go to and how long the journey is likely to take.

It is all a case of what we are used to. If you pick up an average-sized paperback book, you will automatically know that page 203 is somewhere near the back. You can tell the time and make calculations from it; if it is now four o'clock and you are hungry but you know you are not going to have a meal until eight, you will probably decide to have a snack to keep you going.

When dealing with numbers, familiarity is important. That is why so many older people still find it difficult to think in metres, grammes and litres. As children they were taught to use yards, ounces and pints and, having done so for many years, it does not come naturally for them to think in any other way. Although it is now twenty years since decimal coinage was introduced in Britain there are still people who find it difficult to appreciate just how much some of those little coins are worth. Only recently I overheard an elderly lady who had just purchased four stamps in the post office. She handed over one pound and looked in amazement at the few coins she was given as change. 'That's nearly *five shillings* a stamp!' she said. Because she was talking in terms which were familiar to her, she was able to understand the relative values.

Numeracy is not something you do or do not have – although some people do have a natural flair. The ability to grasp the basics of what numbers are telling you is an acquired skill. It is a fact of life that we do not notice the figures we are used to and understand, but are very aware of those we find confusing. This being the case, if you wish to acquire a greater facility with numbers, the only answer is to make yourself familiar with them through repeated practice.

If you want to improve your own numeracy, the next time you are reading a book or an article and you come across figures or a graph stop and look at them – don't simply go on to the next piece of text. Think about the numbers and what they are telling you. You will find it slow and tedious to begin with, but it does become easier the more you do it.

The object of this chapter is not to make you into a brilliant mathematician (indeed I would not be qualified to do so) but to help you to feel at ease with numbers so that they no longer fill you with apprehension. Because numbers play so large a part in our lives, we all need to be able to look at them and understand their significance. And this is far easier than many people at first believe.

Percentages/fractions/decimals

Unless you have a precise calculation to make, it is not always necessary to be able to translate figures shown as percentages into fractions or decimals (or the other way around). But it is useful to be able to glance at those figures and know roughly the amount indicated. If you remember the following examples, you will find it helpful:

$$10\% = \frac{1}{10} = 0.1$$
$$25\% = \frac{1}{4} = 0.25$$
$$50\% = \frac{1}{2} = 0.5$$
$$75\% = \frac{3}{4} = 0.75$$

Now, if you are told that the figure is 16 per cent, you will at once know that it is nearer to $\frac{1}{10}$ than to $\frac{1}{4}$. Similarly, if you are given a figure of 0.8 per cent, you will appreciate that it is more than $\frac{3}{4}$ (or more than 75 per cent).

Calculation

Many people, who might not feel too uncomfortable with numbers themselves, have an absolute horror of calculation. They may know that 8×12 is 96, but what about all those dreadful problems with two trains travelling at different speeds in opposite directions? Yet, once you can see the logic of a problem, much of it reduces to the four basics – addition, subtraction, multiplication and division.

The increased use of calculators may have many advantages, but it does create its own problems too. Because they are now used at such an early stage in a child's life, they often eliminate the familiarity with figures which can only come with constant and repeated practice. More and more people are now leaving school unable to do even the simplest calculations.

Not long ago I was in a department store buying ten items at £2.75 each. Now you and I might know that all you have to do to multiply the £2.75 by ten is move the decimal point one place and put a zero on the end – in other words, £27.50. But not the assistant who was serving me. Slowly and laboriously she punched up on the till £2.75 ten times – or so she thought. When she turned to me and told me the total due was £30.25, it did not strike her that this was impossible and that she must have rung the figure up eleven times instead of ten. She had used mechanical aids to addition for so long that she had no understanding at all of what numbers really meant.

Learning tables

This is something which seems to come into fashion and then depart again, depending upon the education philosophy at the time. But it cannot be denied that, if you know them, it does make life much easier when dealing with numbers. The trouble is that it is extremely boring to stand there and chant: 'Four ones are four; four twos are eight . . .' and so on. One solution is to sing your tables. This is something many children are now being taught to do – indeed, there are even cassettes you can buy for this purpose. But, if you are one of those who find it difficult to give an instant answer to '7 × 9 = ?' or 'What is 6 × 12?', perhaps you could start singing your tables too. After all, very few of us, adult or child, forget the words of a song once we have learned them.

The four basics

For most people who are not going to deal with higher mathematics or differential calculus, all that is needed is to increase their familiarity and dexterity with addition, subtraction, multiplication and division. In each of these areas it is possible to learn methods which are speedier and simpler than those we were probably taught at school.

Addition

Suppose you were asked to add 98 and 97 (without the aid of pen and paper). You may have been taught to say '7 and 8 makes 15, carry the 1 . . .' and so on. But it makes life far easier if you convert the two unfamiliar numbers (98 and 97) into familiar, workable ones (100 and 100). You know that 98 is 2 less than 100, and that 97 is 3 less. You know that $2 + 3 = 5$. Now all you have to say to yourself is $2 \times 100 = 200$; $200 - 5 = 195$.

There are also ways to make use of the fact that it is far simpler to work in modules of 10 than in units of assorted sizes. So, if you are given a column of figures to add, see how many groups of 10 you can make. Suppose you have:

$$9$$
$$3$$
$$6$$
$$2$$
$$7$$
$$8$$
$$4$$
$$1$$
$$\underline{5}$$

Look for any pairs of figures which add up to 10 (putting a mark beside them as you do, so that you do not use any figure twice). This gives you:

$$9 + 1 = 10$$
$$3 + 7 = 10$$
$$6 + 4 = 10$$
$$2 + 8 = 10$$
$$+ 5 = \underline{5}$$
$$\text{total} \quad 45$$

The same thing applies if you have a double column of figures, as shown overleaf:

$$76$$
$$42$$
$$31$$
$$89$$
$$54$$
$$41$$
$$63$$
$$\underline{28}$$

Taking the right-hand column first and using the method shown above, you have:

$$6 + 4 = 10$$
$$2 + 8 = 10$$
$$1 + 9 = 10$$
$$3 + 1 = \underline{4}$$
$$\text{total} \quad 34$$

Then, just as you were taught at school, you carry the 3 over to the left-hand column and repeat the process:

$$7 + 3 = 10$$
$$4 + 6 = 10$$
$$8 + 2 = 10$$
$$4 + 5 = 9$$
$$+ 3 = \underline{3}$$
$$\text{total} \quad 42$$

Your final answer is therefore 424 – and you have not needed to perform acrobatics of addition in your head.

Once you become accustomed to using this method of adding a column of figures – no matter how long it may be or how large the numbers involved – you will find that it cuts the time taken dramatically. Even more significant is that it gives you the confidence to know you are doing it correctly and saves you having to add the same column several times to check that you have not made a mistake.

Whether you enjoyed the experience or not and whether

you found it easy or difficult, you will at some stage of your childhood have learned your tables. Make use of this acquired knowledge when adding a very long column of figures. Notice which numbers occur more than once, and combine these to shorten the column and therefore make mistakes less likely. For instance:

$$
\begin{array}{r}
5 \\
9 \\
4 \\
3 \\
2 \\
7 \\
9 \\
4 \\
1 \\
5 \\
6 \\
9 \\
\underline{2} \\
\end{array}
$$

becomes:

2 × 5	10
3 × 9	27
2 × 4	8
2 × 2	4
3 + 7	10
1 + 6	7
	66

Subtraction

Suppose you want to subtract any number from one ending in a zero, for instance 10, 100, 1000, 10,000, or 100,000. Because of the way children are taught to subtract, this process will usually involve a pen and paper and a long process of 'borrowing' or 'carrying' numbers. Below is a far simpler method which it is quite easy to do in your head. One of the reasons for its simplicity is that it involves working from left to right – the way in which we read – rather than in the opposite direction.

Let us suppose the subtraction with which you are faced is 10,000 – 7146:

Take 1 from 10,000, i.e. 9999, and subtract your figure from this. Then add the 1 to your total.

e.g.
$$\begin{array}{r} 9\ 9\ 9\ 9 \\ -\ 7\ 1\ 4\ 6 \\ \hline 2\ 8\ 5\ 3\ +\ 1 \end{array}$$

So your answer is 2854.

Because all the figures in the top line are 9 and nothing in the bottom line can be higher than 9, you automatically eliminate any carrying or borrowing.

Of course, figures are not always so amenable and, if the number you wish to subtract contains 8s and 9s while the number from which the subtraction is to be made does not, you might well think you are back to carrying again. But this does not have to be so. The important point to remember is that it is so much simpler to work from left to right, so we have to find a way of doing this.

Let us assume the problem is 8392 – 5516. There are just two things to remember:

- where the top number is smaller than the bottom one, add 10 to it
- remember to add 1 to the lower figure which comes immediately to its left. For example:

$$\begin{array}{r} 8\ 3\ 9\ 2 \\ -\ 5\ 5\ 1\ 6 \\ \hline \end{array} \quad \text{becomes} \quad \begin{array}{r} 8\ \ 13\ 9\ 12 \\ \ 6\ \ \ 5\ 2\ \ 6 \\ \hline \end{array}$$

Now it is easy to read your answer from left to right as 2876.

Multiplication

Most of us know how simple it is to multiply by 10 – you just put a 0 on the end of the figure. To multiply by 100, you add two zeros, by 1000 you add three zeros, and so on. If you can do that, you can multiply just as easily by 5, 50, 500 and so on.

To multiply by 5: Multiply by 10 and divide by 2.
e.g. $76391 \times 5 \quad = \quad 763910 \div 2 \quad = \quad 381955$

To multiply by 50: multiply by 100 and divide by 2.
e.g. $46139 \times 50 \quad = \quad 4613900 \div 2 \quad = \quad 2306950$

To multiply by 500: multiply by 1000 and divide by 2.
e.g. $294761 \times 500 \quad = \quad 294761000 \div 2 \quad = \quad 147380500$

The other simple multiplication is by 11. I am sure you already know how to multiply any figure below 10 by 11 – you simply repeat the figure. For example, $7 \times 11 = 77$; and $9 \times 11 = 99$.

When you are faced with a two-figure number it is equally simple. You add the two figures together and insert the total between them.

e.g. $54 \times 11 \quad = \quad 594 \qquad 62 \times 11 \quad = \quad 682$

If those two figures add up to more than 10, add the extra 1 to the figure on the left.

e.g. $39 \times 11 \quad = \quad 429 \qquad 47 \times 11 \quad = \quad 517.$

Division

If multiplying by 5, 50, 500 and so on is easy, so too is division by those numbers. Once again, you use your knowledge of how to divide by 10, 100, 1000.

To divide by 5: divide by 10 and double your answer.
e.g. $976 \div 5 \quad = \quad 97.6 \times 2 \quad = \quad 195.2.$

To divide by 50: divide by 100 and double your answer.
e.g. $3178 \div 50 \quad = \quad 31.78 \times 2 \quad = \quad 63.56$

To divide by 500: divide by 1000 and double your answer
e.g. $427631 \div 500 \quad = \quad 427.631 \times 2 \quad = \quad 855.262.$

Dividing by 2 is simple when you are given numbers like 18, 46 or 24. When the number is a very long one, divide it into segments, each of which is divisible by 2.

e.g. 46327082324 becomes 4 6 32 70 8 2 32 4.
This divides simply and quickly as 2 3 16 35 4 1 16 2
or 23163541162. If the final figure in the original number
is an odd one, you will have to finish with .5 or ½ at the
end.

Remembering numbers

Many people have great difficulty in remembering numbers
with the exception of the few which are important to them.
Indeed, British Telecom did the public no great service
when it decided to abolish words to differentiate exchanges.
It was far easier to remember 'Wembley' or 'Temple Bar'
than three, four or even five seemingly random figures.
Because these numbers in themselves have no particular
meaning, the answer is to translate them into something
which does, something with which we are all familiar –
words.

It is also a fact that we remember most readily anything
which is amusing or even ridiculous. So this is the time to
have a bit of fun while employing a practical method of
number recall.

Suppose you are dealing with telephone numbers. The
first thing you have to do is remember the following code:

1	ABC	6	NO
2	DEF	7	PQ
3	GHI	8	RST
4	JK	9	UVW
5	LM	0	XYZ

(You don't even have to commit this to memory; you can
write it down any time you wish. Just remember that the
first three numbers and the last three numbers each represent three letters of the alphabet, while all the rest represent
only two.)

Now you have to use the relevant letters represented by
the particular figures in a telephone number as the letters of
a word (and in each case you have a choice of letters to
make your word-forming easier).

e.g. 837 8669 might become SIP SNOW, which is far simpler to remember.

If you prefer it, you can use the letters as initials.

e.g. 794 1208 might become Pears with jelly can dry your throat.

Bear in mind that the more ridiculous the phrase, the more likely you are to remember it. So, of course, there is much to be said for linking the words with the owner of that telephone number where possible. For example, if the last number was owned by someone called Valerie, your phrase might be: 'Please Val jump and flex your toes.' I am certain you can think of others for yourself.

Try this exercise. Choose any telephone number you wish and write it here: − − − − − − −

Now the letters (you − − − − − − −

have a choice in each − − − − − − −

case) − − − − − − −

Now have some fun inventing your own words or phrases.

In the same way it is possible to make car registration numbers much more memorable. Continue to work on the theory that words are far easier to remember than random numbers (or even random letters) and, as before, make phrases by converting figures to their equivalent letters of the alphabet.

e.g. If the car number plate reads G472 SAL, you could perhaps use the phrase: 'George, don't go back. Stay and look.'

Of course, if you can find a way of personalising the phrase, it will be even easier to remember. Something along the lines of: 'Gee, Dennis going bald. Shiny and lovely.' (With apologies to any Dennis whose hair may be receding.)

If none of this appeals to you, you could always resort to writing the numbers down but then you have to take care not to lose the piece of paper, to have it with you when you need it, and finally you must remember to look at it. And you won't have nearly as much fun!

If you are one of those people in whom numbers and

calculation have always instilled terror, then it is important to learn to have fun with them. Once you have begun to think of them as sources of amusement or entertainment, you will soon lose your apprehensions and your confidence when working with figures will grow.

There is a simple game you can play, either alone or with another person, which will help increase your facility with numbers. If there are two of you, one person writes down any five numbers of 10 or under and one number between 10 and 100. The other person writes any number between 101 and 999. The object is to see whether, using basic addition, subtraction, multiplication and/or division, you can make the larger number from some or all of the smaller ones. You will be surprised at how often this is possible but, even if it is not, try and see how close you can get. Just as those who regularly play Scrabble develop an 'eye' for word-forming letters, this simple mathematical game will help you to increase your familiarity and adeptness with numbers.

If you wish to play it alone, simply write several numbers of each type on separate pieces of paper. Place them face down or in a bag and select them at random.

By taking a different approach to numeracy, you can certainly learn to make friends of numbers.

10

The End Result

The end result of putting learning techniques into practice will, of course, depend upon your original aim. This chapter is divided into sections on taking exams, making speeches and presentations, and using another language.

Taking exams

The advice in this section applies whether you are taking professional exams, a student at school or college, or studying for the sheer enjoyment of acquiring further knowledge.

Revision and preparation

Of course, if you have been following the suggestions set out in this book, you will have been revising all the time. Every time you make the effort to write out notes, create thought-flow charts or commit information to your long-term memory, you are reviewing and revising. The revision suggestions which follow relate specifically to the run-up time to the exams themselves – and they will come easily to you because you have done most of the groundwork already.

- Don't leave this intensive revision to the last minute, or you will find that you begin to panic. Apart from the fact that this will make relaxation almost impossible, anxiety-related tension reduces your ability to think clearly. As a result, not only will you have less time in which to work, but you are unlikely to make efficient use of whatever time you do have.

- Take the trouble to ensure that you are completely familiar with what you need to know for the forthcoming exam. Check with your tutor or teacher or with the relevant examining body to confirm that you are aware of precisely what is on the syllabus for each subject you are studying. Every exam contains a certain number of compulsory sections and, naturally, these should take priority when you come to work out a revision timetable for yourself.
- Create a revision timetable. Although this will take time and trouble, such time is not wasted. It will ensure that you have a chance to do sufficient work on each subject. To make a good revision timetable:

  1. Decide how much time you have before the exam, and divide this time between the subjects you are studying.
  2. We have already seen that you will remember best what you study at the beginning and end of a revision session, so divide your time into several small study periods rather than a few larger ones.
  3. Never plan to spend an entire day studying a single subject. No matter how much you think you enjoy it, your mind will grow bored and you will cease to be alert enough to take in what you read. As a result you will have to find time to re-revise the same part of the same subject at a later date.
  4. Spend the first revision period of each day studying something you like, or you will find it very hard to settle to it at all. It is amazing how attractive household chores, walking the dog or making coffee can seem when you are not motivated by the first piece of work you have to do.
  5. You are not superhuman, so be sure to leave room in your timetable for food, exercise and leisure activities. Far from wasting some of your precious revision time, it will make you able to work more quickly and effectively.
- Begin each day by making a list of the points you intend to cover in each subject. It is wonderfully satisfying and

gives you a great sense of achievement to cross them off one by one.

- Use all the methods already discussed in this book, as opposed to simply reading and rereading textbooks and notes. Create thought-flow charts which allow your mind to form links between the various pieces of information you have gathered. Draw graphs or diagrams to clarify your ideas. Use visualisation techniques which enable you to become involved in a subject rather than remaining a detached observer.

- Discussion with other students can often prove helpful. Not only will it be a test of your own knowledge, but it may well help you to look at a subject from other points of view or to take a different approach. And bouncing ideas around often brings to light some fact or piece of information previously unknown to you.

- Use a cassette recorder if you have one available. Make a tape of the relevant information and then play it at every opportunity – when you are washing, driving the car or doing any mundane but essential chore. Even if you find yourself 'switching off' and not listening consciously to the spoken words, your subconscious will still hear and accept them. You only have to think of the way many of us remember the lyrics of a popular song after hearing it several times – even if we have never deliberately set out to memorise the words. This technique is particularly effective when learning vocabulary, dates and formulae.

- See if you can obtain some of the exam papers set by the relevant board during previous years so that you may practise working with the type of question and within the appropriate time boundaries they use. Timing yourself at this stage can be really helpful, as it is possible to lose vital marks during an exam if you suddenly run out of time before completing the paper. Don't make the mistake, however, of assuming that, because a certain type of question has come up in three of the past four years, you are bound to be faced with it this year. The examiners may have decided that now is the time to make a change. If you have to take an oral exam, find out what is normally involved and practise speaking for the appropriate amount of time – once again a tape recorder can prove helpful here.

- You will have been reading both required and recommended books throughout your course but, if you can find the time, you can never do too much background reading on any topic related to your studies. It will help you to obtain a more rounded view of the subject. Study Aids are also available in most bookshops. These should not be used in place of compulsory reading, but can be helpful in pointing out the most significant facts.

- Try at this time to be selective in the company you keep. Avoid mixing with those people who are prone to panic – it's catching! Nothing is more likely to make you feel you are unable to cope than listening to others telling you how *they* cannot cope. Similarly, it is not a good idea to spend too much time with depressive people – the type who wring their hands and wonder what on earth they will do if they fail. Remember: positivity begets positivity and negativity begets negativity. And if your own friends or family are inclined to say such things as 'Suppose you don't pass . . .', ask them either to say something supportive or to say nothing at all.

- Try not to revise right up until bedtime, or your brain will be so active that you will find it difficult to sleep. Perhaps you could listen to some music, watch television, go for a walk or have a *warm* bath (too hot or too cold will be a shock to your system and make it harder to relax when you go to bed). Stimulants such as alcohol, pills or excess caffeine are best avoided during the whole of the revision period, but you would certainly do well to give them a miss in the last hour or two before going to bed.

- It is particularly important to maintain a sensible general health regime just before exams. You are likely to be under more pressure than usual, and a healthy lifestyle will make this pressure less likely to have a harmful effect upon you. See that your diet contains all the necessary vitamins and minerals, that you get sufficient rest and that you take regular exercise. Repeated practice of a basic relaxation routine will also help to reduce tension and enable you to concentrate more completely on your work. And remember, as exam time approaches, to set aside a little time each day for the visualisation technique described in Chapter 5.

- Be as organised as possible, both in the revision itself and in your daily life. Constant muddle can be highly stress-inducing and you are trying to reduce the amount of stress upon you at the moment. Establish a routine which is as regular as possible and keep your notes, books and papers in some sort of order. If you do, you will always be able to lay your hands on whatever is required at any moment and will not have to waste precious time searching for some essential piece of information.

- It would be foolish to ask you to avoid all stress just before you take exams; it simply would not be possible. But you can learn to recognise the symptoms when that stress reaches threatening proportions and to take avoiding action. If you find a noticeable and inexplicable change in your eating or sleeping habits, if you find yourself becoming more irritable than usual or if you suddenly become aware of hitherto unknown aches and pains, stress is probably beginning to take hold. STOP! Even if it means taking up some of the time you had allotted to studying, it is more important to deal with the excess stress before it actually does you harm. Practise your relaxation routine and take an hour off to do something pleasurable; you will be able to work doubly hard when you come back to your revision.

- Do you have a calm, no-nonsense and reassuring friend whom you can talk to? Preferably someone who has been in the situation in which you now find yourself. It can be a great help when it comes to putting things into perspective.

- Be true to yourself. There is no point in comparing yourself – whether favourably or unfavourably – to others. You are *you* and, as long as you can honestly say that you are doing your best, no one could ask more of you, whatever the results.

- You will avoid putting yourself under extreme pressure if

you set comparatively small daily goals and keep to them. Great and unattainable goals which you are unable to reach will only make you feel that you are a failure who doesn't stand a chance of passing these exams.

- Promise yourself a special treat once the exams are over. What you choose is a matter of personal preference. You may decide to go on an outing, to buy yourself a present – or to spend the morning in bed. But it is important to give yourself something to look forward to which is in no way dependent on how well you do in the exams themselves.

- It is often easy to lose sight of the fact that everyone wants you to pass these exams – even the examiner. He (or she) does not pick up a paper with hate in his heart and malice in his soul. He is an ordinary person – probably with an ordinary wife and ordinary children – doing a job. His job is to mark your paper, not to see if he can find sufficient reason to fail you.

- Read through all the course work – although, naturally, you cannot know everything about any particular subject. It is up to you to decide how to make the best use of what you do know.

- Be absolutely certain that you fully understand your notes – and, if you have any doubt at all, ask someone. Understanding is a vital part of remembering and, without it, there is no point at all in even entering the exam room.

Be prepared

Your state of mind during an examination begins even before you leave home. In fact, it begins the night before the exam itself.

The evening before

- If the exam is to take place anywhere other than your usual school or college, you should by now have discovered the exact location and your best route for getting there. In fact, you should have made a trial run at the time of day you will be travelling so that you know just how much time to allow for the journey (although, of course, you will allow a little extra to be safe). Remind yourself of the route and make sure you have sufficient small change to pay for the journey.

- Pack your exam bag. Put in everything you need, from pens and pencils to calculators, set squares or anything else appropriate to the exam you will be sitting. It is also a good idea to pack two of everything to allow for loss or breakage or pens running out of ink at an inopportune moment.

- Timing will be vital, so be certain your watch is fully wound or has new batteries, whichever is applicable.

- Have a reasonably – but not ridiculously – early night and prepare for bed slowly, allowing time to enjoy a warm drink or a bath.

- Once you are in bed, practise the relaxation routine to which by now you should have become accustomed. Visualise the exam room and see yourself acting in a positive and confident manner.

- Your mental attitude at this time is of paramount importance and may be linked directly with your eventual result. If you can tell yourself honestly that you have worked hard and, if you will remain as calm as possible in the circumstances, it is highly unlikely that you will fail. Remind yourself of this before you go to sleep.

In the morning
- Get up early enough to allow time for a short walk or a few gentle stretching exercises. These will not only help to ease tension from your body but will clear your head in preparation for the day ahead.

- When you arrive at the exam venue, keep well clear of anyone whom you know is likely to agitate you or cause you to feel anxious. Of course there will be some apprehension within you – that is only natural – but you do not want this to escalate to unmanageable proportions.

- This is not the time for a frantic rereading of your notes: you will only confuse yourself. If you have been studying and revising effectively you will have all the knowledge you need; if you have not studied properly, there is nothing you can do about it now.

- When you reach the exam room itself, sit quietly in your place. Arrange all your pens, pencils and other equipment and put your watch on the desk in front of you where you can see it at a glance. Take a few deep breaths and ease the tension from your neck and shoulders, making sure that your jaw is not tightly clenched.

Exam technique

Essay-type exams

The following hints should help you to do your best in any exam which requires essay-type answers:

- Turn over the paper and read it calmly. What you will probably find is that one particular question springs out at you like an old friend – so at least you know that you have somewhere to start. It is not necessary at this point to study every question in minute detail. It is, however, a good idea to look through the paper and put a tick against those questions you feel you could possibly answer well and – perhaps even more important – a cross against those you definitely do not wish to attempt.
- You are usually allowed to tackle the questions in whatever order you wish, and there are two schools of thought about where to start. One is that you should begin with your best question, as this will help you to feel more confident right from the outset. The other is that it is preferable to begin with your second-best question, because you are likely to feel comparatively confident about this one too. Only then should you proceed to your best question, as by this time you will have got into the swing of things and your thoughts should be flowing easily.
- In an average three-hour essay-type exam you are usually asked to select four questions to answer. Since each question will only carry 25 per cent of the marks, there is no point in spending more than a quarter of the allotted

time on any one of them – however much you may know about the topic given. If you divide the time equally between the questions, you will have forty-five minutes to spend on each. You should be able to allow yourself about five minutes' planning time at the start of each question and a couple of minutes at the end to read through what you have written and make sure you have not left out some vital point. This would still give you just under forty minutes in which to write your answer.

- Take care to answer the question which has been set. You will not be asked to 'write all you know about . . .', so read the question carefully and see what is required of you. You will not gain any extra points, however much background knowledge you have, if you write reams on the wrong aspect of the topic.

- On your exam paper, underline the key words in the question; words such as 'describe', 'compare', 'evaluate' or 'contrast'. That way you can be sure you know what is required of you, and you will be far less likely to approach the subject from the wrong angle.

- Unless it specifically states otherwise, you will be expected to present arguments for and against what is implied by the question. Be as objective as possible; this is not the time to stand on your own soapbox.

- Spend part of your five minutes' preparation time jotting down some one-word notes concerning ideas from your course which the question brings to your mind. In this way you are less likely to leave out any one aspect altogether. It also allows you time to decide what to include in your answer and what to leave out.

- On your written paper, just put the question number; don't waste time by rewriting the entire question.

- Structure your written answer by giving it a beginning, a middle and an end and dividing it properly into paragraphs.

- Use information gleaned from the course. Naturally you can add supplementary facts gained from your own background knowledge, but the examiner will expect to be able to tell from your answer that you have studied this particular course. You can help to prove this by including such phrases as 'as X points out . . .' to show that you are not simply stating your own opinion.

- Whatever happens, don't be tempted to waffle or to pad out your answer; it will be instantly spotted and you will not gain anything by it. It is better to give a concise answer containing all the essential facts.

- As part of the ongoing learning process, you should have ensured that your spelling and grammar were of sufficiently high standard. There are those who believe that such details do not matter in an exam, but any examiner will tell you that this is not the case. The occasional spelling mistake may be forgiven, but *never* if you misspell a word which actually appears on the question paper. And you really cannot afford to throw away marks.

- Be aware of your handwriting and the quality of your presentation. A genius will not fail because of a poor layout, but you want to make it as easy as possible for the examiner to read what you have written. Bear in mind that each examiner will be reading vast numbers of papers and will not have time to stop and decipher writing which is virtually illegible. You don't need to be fanatical about your presentation; simply pay a little attention to it.

- If the paper requests that you 'Answer only four questions' and you answer five, only the first four will be taken into account when marking. If you are asked to 'Answer either A or B' you may naturally answer whichever you prefer. If you answer both, however, only the first one you tackle will be taken into account.

- Try and keep to your plan as you work. Return to the question in your conclusion; this will help you to keep in mind what is being asked of you.

- If you have been following your plan you should have sufficient time to spend on each question. Suppose, however, you reach the last question and find that you have no time left in which to write a full answer. It is better at this point to make a list, in note form, of the points you would have covered than to write a detailed first half and no second half at all.

- When you have finished writing you should still have

time to read through your paper and correct any glaring mistakes.

- Remember that far more people fail exams because of nervous tension than for any lack of knowledge. If you find that you are beginning to panic, stop for a moment, breathe deeply, relax your jaw and then continue.

Mathematics exams

- In this instance you do not need to read through the entire paper first. Just start at the beginning and work through the questions in order.
- It is essential to read the questions carefully so that you do what is required of you.

Multiple-choice papers

- In a multiple-choice exam, work steadily through the paper answering all those questions you can cope with instantly and leaving out the others. Then go back afterwards to those you have left out.
- Study all your options in a multiple-choice question rather than jumping to immediate conclusions.
- When you reach the end, and provided you still have time, study those questions you have been unable to answer. If you are totally nonplussed, take a guess. In multiple-choice exams there is no point in leaving a question unanswered as you will then score no marks at all for that particular one. It is better to take a chance on a lucky guess.

Once the exams are over

Whatever those around you do, try and avoid indulging in post-mortems. You are bound to think of things you have omitted or mistakes you have made – whether you have actually done so or not. And to concentrate on all the negative aspects of the exam will only depress you.

If you have several weeks to wait until the results are available, do all that you can to fill your mind with other things. There is absolutely nothing you can do about the exams now that they are over and done with, so this is the time to start a new project, meet your friends or take up a fresh hobby.

Remember that treat you promised yourself once all the hard work and the trauma were over? Well, now is the time to enjoy it.

Making speeches and presentations

For many reasons, nothing is more boring for an audience than watching someone reading a previously written speech:

1. The words written may not always be entirely appropriate, but the speaker is unlikely to change them to suit the particular situation or audience.
2. The speaker's head will be down so that he (or she) can read the written notes, and as a result the voice may be muffled and the words difficult to distinguish. If he tries to avoid this situation by holding the paper up in front of him, the audience will not be able to see the expression on his face.
3. The speaker will tend to deliver his words in a monotone, as he will be more concerned with reading his notes than with their content and meaning.
4. Because he has to remain in a position from which he is able to read his notes, the speaker is unlikely to vary his movement or expression.
5. Should he lose his place when reading, drop the piece of paper or mistakenly turn two pages at once, not only will the speaker be embarrassed but he is unlikely to be able to continue effectively as he will have no ongoing train of thought to pursue.

So, for a speech or presentation to be successful, it has to be learned. This does not negate the value of writing it out in full first. Doing so will enable you to check your facts and ensure that your speech is well structured and contains all that you wish to say.

Once you are satisfied with what you have written, read it aloud to ensure that it is neither too long nor too short for the time you have to fill. Reading it aloud will also enable you to confirm that it flows well and will be interesting to your audience.

Never attempt to memorise your speech word for word. Not only will it sound false when you give it but, if you happen to lose your place, you will flounder hopelessly. Presumably you are familiar with the subject about which you are going to talk (you do not really have the right to be talking about it at all if you are not), so you should be able to follow a plan without actually learning a script.

Although you should not have the whole speech written out in front of you, it is often useful to write key words or sentences on small (5 × 3 in) cards; these can serve as 'memory-joggers' and enable you to give your speech a coherent structure. It is quite acceptable to use these cards, which are small enough to be held in the hand without limiting your movement in any way. And since you only need to glance at them from time to time you are able to maintain eye contact with your audience.

Because the cards will contain reminders of what you wish to say rather than the precise words you intend to employ, use them when you rehearse your speech. And rehearse you must. To boost your own confidence, it is a good idea to learn by heart the opening sentence of your talk; this helps to overcome natural nervousness and tension caused by the occasion. You might also wish to learn by heart the closing sentence, so that you do not have to mutter vaguely, 'Well, er, I think that's all I wanted to say. . . .'

When you are rehearsing, utter your speech aloud even if you are alone. Not only will this help you to keep to your allocated time, but words reviewed by being spoken are actually easier to remember than those simply read. Remember to use all the emphasis and expression you hope to command when giving your final performance.

Using another language

There is the world of difference between reading and learning another language in theory and actually using it in practice. And yet, the majority of those who study a foreign language do so to be able to speak (and sometimes write) in a way which will be understood by those with whom they are communicating.

The greatest barrier to using another language is fear – fear of being misunderstood and fear of looking foolish as we struggle to find the right words. But the important thing to remember is that people take it as a compliment if you make even a faltering attempt to speak to them in their own language. And, just as you would be willing to help someone who was having difficulty with English, you will almost always find that others will be eager to help you.

The sooner you are able to build up your confidence the better, so don't be afraid to have a go. Avoid the temptation to make your first sentence: 'Parlez-vous anglais?' or 'Sprechen Sie Englisch?' If the answer is 'Yes', you will have lost a golden opportunity and all that learning will have been in vain.

If you have been learning a language so that you can manage when travelling abroad on holiday, it matters not if you speak in single words to begin with. After all, if a foreigner were to walk into a baker's shop in England, point to a sticky bun and utter the word 'cake', he would get what he wanted. There is no reason why you cannot do the same in another country.

Travelling abroad has another advantage, of course – you will hear the language all around you, see it on the advertisement hoardings and road signs and over shop doorways. As you travel along, say these words to yourself – fill your mind with the language. The meanings will usually be obvious because of the pictures on the billboards or the goods in the shops.

If you are studying a language so that your business can expand into Europe (or elsewhere), there will be certain standard phrases you need to know. Because the phrases will apply to your own business, it should not be too difficult to visualise the object to which the new words and phrases relate. If you are a widget manufacturer and you learn the Italian for 'upper widget section' and 'lower widget section', use the words as often as possible. Write them on drawings of the relevant parts of the widget; stick labels on a widget and keep it on your desk. Even if you do not consciously look at those labels, your subconscious mind will be aware of the words written upon them.

So, whatever your reason for wanting to learn another language, the sooner you begin to use it the better.

Of course, the end result of your learning may not be one of those illustrated in this chapter. But it is possible to adapt the advice set out here to the majority of situations. Writing, even if not for an exam, requires the same planning process. Speaking, even if not making a presentation or using a foreign language, demands the same rehearsal, practice and confidence building. So use the techniques described here and make all that learning worth while.

11

Step by Step to Learning

You now have sufficient information and techniques at your fingertips to enable you to learn effectively and to improve your memory and recall ability. What follows is a résumé which is designed to consolidate those basic essentials so that they are readily available.

The three stages of learning

- Absorption of new ideas
- Blending of new information with what you already know
- Ability to explain what you know

Left and right brain

- Find out whether you are predominantly left- or right-brained
- Try and achieve a balance between the two

External influences on the brain

- *Nutrition* – ensure you have a balanced diet
- *Stimulants* – avoid excess caffeine, alcohol, tobacco and drugs
- *Physical activity* – take a reasonable amount of exercise
- *Conditioning* – don't allow the past to put barriers in your path
- *Stress* – practise breathing, relaxation and so on.

Setting the stage for learning

- Make the place (kept just for studying if possible) comfortable
- Know whether you are a lark or an owl
- Plan your time realistically
- Take frequent breaks to refresh your mind and stretch your body
- Divide your studying into small chunks – remember you absorb best what you learn at the start and end of a session

Becoming a more creative thinker

- Practise listing as many uses as possible for any household object such as a matchstick or a paper clip
- Use brainstorming to help solve problems
- Bear in mind that there may be more than one solution to any problem
- Don't be afraid to fail; it is all part of the learning process
- It is always possible to work your way around obstacles
- Never reject an idea just because it is different
- Remember that the easiest route is not always the best
- Work at developing your imaginative powers
- Practise visualising
- Create thought-flow charts
- Increase the opportunities for creativity in your everyday life by taking up a hobby or allowing yourself to daydream
- Believe that *everyone* is capable of learning

The three stages of memory

- Immediate
- Short-term
- Long-term

To convert from short-term to long-term memory

- You must want to remember
- Repetition or review
- Committal

About memory

- There is no limit to what you can remember
- You need to be motivated and to keep your goals in mind
- There is a difference between visual and verbal memory. Which one comes more naturally to you? Try to improve the other aspect.
- To remember something, you must understand it fully in the first place
- Reinforce your understanding (use highlighters, diagrams and other aids)
- Rehearse and review the facts several times at lengthening intervals
- Recall is the ability to retrieve stored information

Aids to memory

- Try and see a logical pattern in the facts
- Speak the facts aloud
- Use cassettes to help you
- Work together with a friend so that you can test each other on your knowledge
- Make full use of your imagination
- Use thought-flow charts to test your memory
- Take frequent breaks to avoid fatigue
- Don't try and remember facts in isolation. Blend them with what you already know.
- Anything amusing or ridiculous is easier to remember
- Learn things in groups or sequences
- Use rhymes or mnemonics to help you

Seeing

- Understand the difference between seeing and observing
- Practise observation tests (pretend to be a police witness or try and remember objects on a tray).
- Don't 'see' something just because you expect it to be there

Visualisation

- Everyone can visualise – it just takes regular practice
- Follow the exercises to improve your ability to visualise

Uses of visualisation

- As an aid to relaxation
- Helps in the transfer of information to the long-term memory
- Assists recall
- Is valuable in overcoming exam nerves
- As a way of remembering names and faces
- As a way of remembering lists and random items

Hearing

- Understand the difference between hearing and listening
- Practise listening skills and exercises
- Take notes while listening – but not too many. It is more important to understand.
- If you think you may not have understood, ask questions

Improving your reading

- Understand how your eyes work and how you read
- Increase your reading speed by:
    - practising timing test pieces
    - controlling your eye movement
    - using a pointer

Reading to learn

- Set the scene by:
    - having adequate lighting
    - being comfortable
    - being in the right state of mind
- Before starting, look through the book at the contents, headings, index and so on
- Divide what you are to study into workable modules
- Stop and think regularly in order to blend new facts with what you already know
- Make notes as you read
- Be interested in what you are reading
- Pick out key words as you go along

Possible sticking points

- Fatigue
- You have set yourself too great a task
- The text is too difficult (ask for help or try another book)
- The vocabulary is unfamiliar – look up any words which appear regularly

After a reading session

- Think about what you have read
- Write your notes
- Create a thought-flow chart

Eye exercises

- Practise regularly during periods of intense study

Writing

- Practise frequently in order to increase your speed
- Use the correct materials
- Try abbreviations or excluding vowels and any other time- and effort-savers

Note-taking

- Always include a date, title and any other salient information
- Listen to what is being said and make sure you understand it
- Establish a writing rhythm and try to keep it going. If you miss something, leave a gap and find out what it was later
- Rewrite your notes as soon as possible

Rewriting

- Leave spaces for the insertion of future information
- Use diagrams, graphs and thought-flow charts
- Always keep full details of your sources
- Make facts stand out by using headings, sub-headings and coloured highlighters
- Follow the lecturer's structure
- Update your notes frequently as you gain more knowledge

Writing essays

- The gathering of information is as important as the writing of the essay, so allow time for this
- Consider the restrictions (time allowed, number of words required and so on) before you begin
- Think carefully about what is being asked for in the title. Understand what is meant by such words as 'discuss' and 'compare'.
- Make a plan
- Divide into (1) introduction, (2) main body and (3) conclusion
- Suit your language to the type of work
- Take care with grammar, spelling and punctuation
- Make your essay readable
- Refer back to the title in the conclusion

- Write a first draft, then read and correct it
- Make a final copy

Working with numbers

- Don't be frightened of them. You already deal with them more than you realise in your daily life.
- Play games to increase your familiarity with numbers
- Practise exercises to make work simpler in the four basics – addition, subtraction, multiplication and division

Remembering numbers

- Convert to letters or words where possible

Examinations

- There are four stages: revision, preparation, exam technique and when it is all over

Revision

- Allow plenty of time before the exam
- Check up on what you need to know
- Make a revision timetable
- List what you intend to cover each day, and take pleasure in crossing out items when completed
- Make charts and diagrams to help you
- Discuss the subject with others
- Use cassettes as an aid
- Practise old exam papers
- Do as much background reading as time permits
- As exams approach, avoid people who have a tendency to panic
- Never revise right up until bedtime
- Look after your general health
- Keep both your notes and your daily life as well organised as possible
- Set yourself small goals and keep to them

Preparation

- Promise yourself a treat to be enjoyed once the exams are over
- Bear in mind that everyone wants you to pass
- Make sure you are familiar with the place where the exam is to take place
- Keep an exam bag packed and ready
- Check that your watch is working
- Have a reasonably early night just before an exam
- Practise relaxation and visualisation in bed

On the day

- Get up in time for a good breakfast and a small amount of exercise
- Avoid those who cause you to feel agitated
- Don't reread your notes at this stage – it will only confuse you or cause you anxiety
- Once in the exam room, arrange your materials and your watch. Practise a breathing exercise.

Essay-type exams

- Read through the paper and mark those questions you intend to answer
- Begin with either your best or second-best question
- Allow five minutes' planning time per question
- Allow time to read through at the end
- Answer the precise question set
- Underline key words on the question paper
- In your planning time, write one-word notes
- Structure your answer to include a beginning, middle and end
- Use information gleaned from the course
- Use quotations for credibility where possible
- Don't waffle
- Take care with handwriting, spelling, grammar and presentation

- Only answer the number of questions required of you
- Keep to your outline plan
- If you run out of time, write your final answer in note form
- Should you begin to panic, stop for a moment and regulate your breathing

Maths exams

- Don't bother to read the paper all the way through first. Work through the questions in order.
- Read each question carefully so that you know what is being asked of you

Multiple-choice exams

- Work steadily through, answering all the questions you can and omitting what you cannot do at once
- Make sure you study all the options
- When you have answered all the questions you know, go back and work your way through the ones you did not know
- If you are really stuck, guess

After the exams are over

- Avoid indulging in post-mortems
- If you have some time to wait before the results, fill your time with something new and interesting
- Enjoy the treat you promised yourself

Remembering speeches or presentations

- Write your speech in full first, but *never* read from a script on the day
- Read your written speech aloud to yourself
- Prepare key cards
- Make sure you know your subject

- Learn your opening and closing sentences by heart
- Rehearse well

Using a foreign language

- Take every opportunity to use the language
- Don't be afraid to use single words to begin with
- If abroad, absorb the language surrounding you
- Fix labels with the correct translations to the relevant objects

Further Information

Additional reading

Michele Brown, *How to Study Successfully for Better Exam Results* (Sheldon Press, 1990)
Tony Buzan, *Make the Most of Your Mind* (Pan, 1977)
Harry Lorayne, *How to Develop a Super-Power Memory* (Signet, 1974)
Ursula Markham, *Elements of Visualisation* (Element Books, 1989)
Edward de Bono, *De Bono's Thinking Course* (BBC Books, 1982)
Gordon Wainwright, *Rapid Reading Made Simple* (W.H. Allen, 1972)
Betty Edwards, *Drawing on the Right Sight of the Brain* (Fontana, 1982)

Self-help audio cassettes are available from

The Hypnothink Foundation
PO Box 154
Cheltenham
Glos GL53 9EG

Thorsons
77–85 Fulham Palace Road
London W6 8JB

Index